Twayne's United States Authors Series

Sylvia E. Bowman, *Editor*

INDIANA UNIVERSITY

Margaret Fuller

MARGARET FULLER

by **ARTHUR W. BROWN**

Utica College of Syracuse University

 48

Twayne Publishers, Inc.   ::   New York

To Patricia
WHO ALSO KNOWS HER OWN MIND

"Margaret had so many aspects to her soul, that she might furnish material for a hundred biographers, and all would not be said even then."

—James F. Clarke

Preface

THE GREAT LAWSUIT of which Margaret Fuller wrote with such verve more than a century ago in *The Dial*, the "little magazine" of the New England transcendentalists, still remains unsettled. Though it appears now to be cold war rather than open conflict, the battle of the sexes is still being waged. Both sexes continue to call for fairer play, but no one speaks with greater vehemence or authority today than a voice from out of the past. More than a century ago, in her much celebrated *Woman in the Nineteenth Century* and throughout a varied career of trial and achievement, Margaret Fuller set for herself the difficult goal of vindicating woman's birthright. Sadly enough, few moderns have read the book which Horace Greeley claimed had "the real stuff in it"; and even fewer know the warm, flesh-and-blood woman with heart equal to mind and the firm conviction that "character is higher than intellect."

Scholarly thoroughness and dedication have done much in the past twenty-five years to map and investigate the cultural milieu and to identify major personalities of the transcendentalist movement. Emerson, Thoreau, and Hawthorne have been richly served, but lesser figures like George Ripley, Orestes Brownson, and the Channing cousins still await their turn. So does Margaret Fuller. The handiwork of early biographer-friends and the tributes of later feminists have created a mixed portrait of peculiarity and contradictions. Sibyl or sinner? Bluestocking? Genius or fraud? Egomaniac? Which, if any, is the true image? The truth, as always, lies somewhere in between.

And so the need to take a closer look at the woman Poe labeled out of sheer pique a "detestable old maid"; whom Hawthorne maligned as a "strong and coarse nature"; and for whom Horace Greeley prescribed "a good husband and two or three bouncing babies" as an antidote to a lot of "cant and nonsense." And there is profit also in following the ups and downs of Emerson's determined efforts to know the different faces of Margaret's "mountainous me." It is obvious that Poe's disdain for the world of "Frogpondium" and its "servile imitators of the English" colored his judgment of Miss Fuller. We shall never know why charity failed Hawthorne when he sat in judgment on his companion of happier days in Concord's Sleepy Hollow, but he should not be blamed for the poor taste of his son, who violated the privacy of a personal journal. Horace Greeley, we discover, was man enough, despite billy-goat stubbornness, to own finally that woman's ability and will might enable her to play several roles successfully.

These are but a few of the personal questions that should provoke interest concerning the life and influence of Margaret Fuller. But of even greater importance are the roles that she played as an interpreter of European culture to America and as a genuine critic and supporter of an improved literature that should give voice to the aspirations of a nation destined one day to become great. To do justice to these roles and to evaluate their significance, I have established several aims for the present study, not the least of which is to wipe out the impression that Margaret Fuller belonged to a kind of third sex because she dared to use her mind and to speak on topics upon which there was a conspiracy of silence. When a distinguished modern scholar can still write, "Margaret Fuller could actually think better than a great many men," it is reasonable to infer that "actually" implies a kind of "Gee whiz!" performance. With every intent to reject such an implication, I have accepted Margaret Fuller's radicalism at face value as deriving from the premises of her argument that Man encompasses both man and woman, a fact that requires no special stress to be laid on the welfare of either. She represents the essentially revolutionary nature of the transcendental metaphysic and is in many ways a better exponent of action wedded to idea than her better-known contemporaries.

Margaret Fuller's efforts at versification and prose composition contain none of the personal magnetism and electrifying enthusiasm of her conversation. She called her verses "vents for the overflowing of a personal experience," the normal practice in an age of sensibility; and I see no reason to question her critical acumen. Publication of her prose thoughts was an "auction of the soul" to which she submitted only because the public's need outweighed private consideration. Although she rarely had time or opportunity to polish her writing, I have found no evidence to prove that she ever developed any distinction as a stylist. There is progress but no fulfillment. Really memorable expression is to be found only occasionally in her letters and journals. She is proof once again that great talkers seldom earn renown with their pens.

Libraries are still being turned over to make books, and I have tried to identify in notes and bibliography the sources that have broadened and clarified my thinking about Margaret Fuller. My undertaking has been made possible by the help and cooperation of many people and several institutions. To the American Council of Learned Societies for its generous grant and to Syracuse University for a sabbatical leave to use it, I am indeed grateful. To Dorothy Judd Sickels for her generous help and to my colleagues who have taken up the slack and to Utica College's efficient library staff, my special thanks. For her editorial assistance and for entrusting a woman's reputation to my care, Sylvia Bowman deserves special credit. The staff of the Boston Public Library and the Harvard College Library have been of inestimable help in lightening the burden of research. Thanks are due also to the personnel of the New York Public Library and the J. Pierpont Morgan Library for their courteous assistance. I am grateful also for help received from the Hamilton College Library and from the public libraries of Concord and Cambridge, Massachusetts, and Utica, New York. For permission to quote from manuscript sources in their possession, I wish finally to thank William H. Jackson, Houghton Library; John Alden, Curator of Rare Books, Boston Public Library; and John D. Gordan, Curator of the Berg Collection, New York Public Library.

ARTHUR W. BROWN

Utica, New York
December, 1962

Contents

Chronology

1810   Sarah Margaret Fuller, eldest of nine children of Timothy and Margaret Crane Fuller, is born at Cambridgeport, Mass., May 23.

1823-   Student at Misses Prescott's school, Groton, Mass.
1824

1824-   Flowering in Cambridge. Companion and confidante of
1833   several members of Harvard Class of 1829 and Divinity School Class of 1833: William Henry Channing, James Freeman Clarke, Frederick Henry Hedge.

1833   Rustication on Groton farm. Teaches younger children of family: Arthur, Ellen, Richard, Lloyd.

1835   Timothy Fuller dies; Margaret becomes breadwinner and head of family.

1836   First visit to the Emersons in Concord and beginning of lifelong correspondence and friendship with Waldo.

1836-   Teacher in Bronson Alcott's Temple School. Gives private
1837   instruction in German and Italian.

1837-   Teacher in Hiram Fuller's Greene Street School, Provi-
1839   dence, R.I. Translates *Eckermann's Conversations with Goethe* (1839).

1839   Moves family from Groton to Jamaica Plain and takes upon herself burdens as head of the house. Begins Conversation classes in Boston and Cambridge, which continue until 1844.

1840   Edits *The Dial* from July of this year until July, 1842.

1841   Brook Farm started. Margaret and Emerson are well-wishers but prize individuality too much to join the "association."

1842   Publishes her translation of *Correspondence of Fräulein Günderode and Bettina von Arnim.*

1843   Western trip with James and Sarah Clarke.

1844   Publishes *Summer on the Lakes*, an account of her "westering," which attracted the attention of Horace Greeley and was partially responsible for his offering her the job of literary critic for the New York *Daily-Tribune.* Goes to New York in December.

1845   Meets James Nathan in February and falls deeply in love. Publication of *Woman in the Nineteenth Century*, an expanded version of the July, 1843, article in *The Dial*, "The Great Lawsuit: Man vs. Men, Woman vs. Women."

1846   Publication of *Papers on Literature and Art*, a miscellany of critical articles. Sails for Europe in August with Marcus and Rebecca Spring. Learns of Nathan's engagement to a German girl. Travels in England, Scotland, and France; acts as foreign correspondent for Greeley's *Tribune*.

1847   Arrives in Rome and meets a young Italian nobleman, the Marchese Ossoli, who offers his love. Leaves Rome to travel in northern Italy and Switzerland. Returns in the autumn and accepts Ossoli. Marriage takes place secretly either in late winter or early spring after Margaret discovers she is to have a child.

1848   Leaves Rome and spends summer in the Abruzzi at Aquila and Rieti while she waits for child. Her son Angelo born on September 5.

1849   Roman Republic proclaimed in February. Margaret with Ossoli during siege of Rome by French in April, May, and June. Appointed director of a hospital and cares for wounded. Reveals the existence of her husband and child to Mrs. Emelyn Story. Writes home to family and friends of marriage. News excites gossip that still colors contemporary accounts.

1850   Goes to Florence after the Republic falls. Sails for America with husband and child on May 17. All three perish in shipwreck at Fire Island, July 19.

1852   Publication of *Memoirs of Margaret Fuller Ossoli* by devoted friends Ralph Waldo Emerson, W. H. Channing, and J. F. Clarke.

Margaret Fuller

CHAPTER 1

A Queen Anne's Man and His Heir

> "I am confident I should have been much
> superior to myself had sense, intellect,
> affection, passion been brought out in
> natural order." [1]—M.F.

WAKEFUL AND RESTLESS as Fancy, the life of Margaret Fuller is a promise of great things never to be fully accomplished. Sooner than most she selected a high goal for life's journey and never lost sight of the way that it pointed. From first to last, her aim was self-culture. "Very early," she writes, "I knew that the only object in life was to grow." [2] She had largely her father to thank for this direction. Before she was ten, he admonished her, "To excel in all things should be your constant aim; mediocrity is obscurity." [3] Later, her reading of Goethe lent substance to her father's advice. Ever onward, like Schiller, she pursued fulfillment as a law of her being. When she encountered circumstances too stubborn for will to overcome, she found consolation in a lesson learned only with grief and pain. She accepted the need we all must feel at times "to change the *nature* of our self-reliance." Although she recognized that man was powerless to determine his exact mode of existence, she firmly believed in an "immutable essence" behind the façade of action, and she faced life with the conviction that she could live by its light.

Like Henry Adams, born to be a child of the nineteenth century and fitted for that life with an eighteenth-century inheritance, she rebelled against acceptance of her lot and that of women in general. That rebellion led eventually to concerted effort and major victories by feminist leaders; but its immediate effect was to bring her out of the somewhat yeasty air of New England into the workaday world of New York journalism, where she could plant herself firmly athwart the path of the world's misery. But her involvement was still too indirect. Restless and filled with the fires of unquenched passion, she sailed for Europe and the scenes and people she knew only through the pages of literature. There she found both love and a cause into which she could pour her entire being. In the role of wife and mother and in the struggle of the Roman Republic to be born, she found release for the "Italy glowing beneath the Saxon crust." But the Republic strangled in its birth pangs, and the long journey home to America ended in a watery grave for the entire Ossoli family. With the inevitability of classic drama, Margaret Fuller's life moved to its tragic conclusion in the aftermath of fallen hopes of liberty. She would have hated anticlimax.

I *The First Bias*

Lawyer Timothy Fuller was a strong-willed man who liked things his own way. But he had had long experience with adversity, and he was not entirely surprised when his first-born turned out to be a girl. He had determined on a son, but he accepted the newcomer with considerable grace and planned to bring her up as though she were a boy. Sarah Margaret Fuller was born on May 23, 1810, the first daughter and the eldest of nine children that Margaret Crane Fuller was to bear.[4] Ten years younger than her husband, the daughter of Major Peter Crane of Canton, Massachusetts, was a "fair and flower-like nature" to be united with one of the "fighting" Fullers. But, despite his rather domineering spirit, Timothy had his gentler side, and their marriage in 1809 was often happy as well as fruitful.

Cherry Street in Cambridgeport, where Margaret Fuller grew up, was only a short distance from Harvard Yard and the Lowells of Brattle Street, although on the social scale the difference in worlds could easily be measured. Timothy Fuller came from several generations of good New England stock; but the Fuller clan had never been yea-sayers, and rebellion had resulted in loss of status down through the years. First place at Commencement in 1801 had gone to another because of Timothy's participation in one of the student rebellions at Harvard, and he further proved his independence the same year by casting his first presidential vote for Jefferson. He was, moreover, a Unitarian.

Socially and politically, then, Timothy Fuller stood somewhat apart from the center of the Boston and Cambridge universe. But politics was in his blood, and he chose the law as the surest way to political preferment. In 1804 he had been admitted to the Massachusetts bar, and hard work led to his election as a representative to Congress in 1817. Eight years later, he became Speaker of the Massachusetts House.

When Margaret was scarcely more than a baby, Timothy Fuller took charge of his daughter's training. Because his wife was often ill, even during the times when she was not pregnant, he gradually turned to his daughter for companionship. A second daughter, born in 1812, might have changed the family picture. But she died shortly after birth, and Margaret remained an only child until Eugene was born in 1815. By then a pattern was beginning to develop. Timothy Fuller was resolved on making his daughter "heir of all he knew" and of as much more as she could possibly absorb.

With the same zest for learning that had driven him to excel at Harvard, he centered his attention on the child's education. A man of business, even in literature, and a "Queen Anne's man" where English literature was concerned, Lawyer Fuller prized high standards, accuracy, and precision. He drove his daughter too rapidly during the days and kept her waiting upon him evenings until he could find time to hear her lessons. The result was foregone. A sensitive temperament and a keen intellect were abnormally stimulated. Margaret became a prodigy of learning, but she paid a severe price in headaches, a nervous stomach, insomnia, and nightmares.

More harmful even than these physical symptoms was the emotional damage. Margaret fell prey to morbid imaginings about death and grew neurotic in behavior. It would take a D. H. Lawrence or a Thomas Mann, perhaps, to do justice to the influences radiating from these experiences of childhood; but Margaret herself, at the age of thirty, showed remarkable insight into her emotional history. Although she could not fathom completely the conflicts that had cloaked themselves in vivid dreams, she more than half suspected that her earlier reasons for thinking dreams "more real" than her conscious activities stemmed from her unwillingness to accept at face value her relationship with her father.[5]

Margaret's serious education began when she was six. She was taught English and Latin grammar and began then to read Latin authors, a daily practice followed for years. Her father, who found Roman *virtus* a model for character-building, fed her a steady diet of Horace and Virgil; and through the eyes of Ovid she looked into "the enchanted gardens" of Grecian mythology. From the Romans she learned to prize the importance of will and resolve. "It never shocks us that the Roman is self-conscious," she wrote. "One wants no universal truths from him, no philosophy, no creation, but only his life. . . ." [6] Here was fostered the disdain for metaphysics that in later years prevented her from following the flights of thinkers like Fichte and Jacobi. [7] Her approach to Grecian culture was largely unphilosophical also. Mythology provided the key because she never mastered the language. Identifying beauty as the law of Grecian life, she found in moderation the law that had enabled the Greeks to court the goddess so successfully.

Since there were no childish companions to dispel the loneliness of these early years, Margaret found her only refuge from the world of studies in the small garden behind the Fuller house. There she dreamed away the hours and gave loving attention to the flowers that her mother had planted. Resolving to be as beautiful as these fragrant blooms, she showed the beginning of that tendency to sentimentalize nature and to identify herself with natural forms that shows in so much of the verse that she wrote in later years. Whatever its effect on her, the practice was one that Timothy Fuller would have put a stop to, if he had taken time to find out about it.

A reader of wide-ranging taste himself, Margaret's father knew the value of reading for pleasure as well as for profit. When lessons were done, Margaret was encouraged to delve for treasure in the book-filled closet that served as the Fuller library. Many an hour glided magically away as she sat book in hand, reading or pensively looking out the closet window at the range of blue hills sloping away from the open countryside. Like young Tom Wolfe imagining enfabled regions beyond the mountains encircling Asheville, Margaret lost herself in visions of foreign lands and romantic adventures, as fancy touched the pages of her books. She read the French Jacobins and the Queen Anne favorites of her father and ploughed through the pages of Smollett and Fielding, but the realism of the novelists offended her sense of the fastidious. As a matter of fact, she never overcame this feeling because her admiration for Balzac's adherence to truth was tempered, in later years, by a feeling of revulsion toward his fidelity of detail.[8] Ever the romantic where taste was concerned, she could heroically face the sternest realities when life called for action.

Three giants loomed on her reading horizon while she was still a little girl. She encountered Shakespeare at eight and met with her father's displeasure by reading *Romeo and Juliet* on the Sabbath. Cervantes followed soon after, and she discovered in this lesser genius the same lessons of quixoticism that later intrigued and lent formal value to the writings of F. Scott Fitzgerald and Ernest Hemingway. Molière made up the other major influence. All three were alike in recording the "natural history of man," the story of man as he *is*, not as he should be. They taught her "to distrust all invention . . . not based on a wide experience," a valuable lesson for one who would one day become a journalist but perhaps more injurious than helpful to one who wished to cultivate the shaping power of imagination.

When Margaret was thirteen, she made the acquaintance of a lovely English visitor to Cambridge. The beauty and grace of the older woman overwhelmed the impressionable youngster, who began to worship her every word and action. There had never been anyone quite like the glamorous stranger in Margaret's life, and her departure left the child inconsolable. For the first time, Timothy Fuller began to realize that his daughter was developing without the kind of companions and influences that a growing girl needs. He decided to send her away to school, and he chose the country town of Groton, Massachusetts, as a proper change of scenery. He enrolled her in the school operated by Susan Prescott and her sister, and Margaret spent her fourteenth and fifteenth years there.

How far she had come to differ from other girls her age was soon brought home to Margaret by some of the experiences that she had at the Prescott seminary for young ladies. She gave a thinly veiled autobiographical account of them when she wrote *Summer on the Lakes* twenty years later. Mariana, the heroine of that account, was undoubtedly Margaret herself; and Mariana's difficulties in trying first of all to win over her classmates to her dislike for routine and discipline and later to impress them by her bizarre antics and theatrical manners were also Margaret's.

Admiration for Mariana's electrifying ways gave way eventually to school-girl disenchantment and a conspiracy to put her in her place. A stoic front before the group shattered in convulsions behind the closed door of her room and later changed into a campaign to sow discord in the school. When she was finally brought to face the accusations of the girls whose character she had tried to damage, she fell down and dashed her head against the iron hearth and was carried to her room senseless.

For several days Mariana neither spoke nor ate. At first she could think of nothing but her own sense of injury. Gradually, however, she began to realize that she had acted very badly. But despair filled her thoughts; surely she was too evil to be saved. The catalyst to dissolve her guilt was provided by an understanding teacher who confided to her a similar experience during her own adolescence. Much chastened, Mariana became a different person and soon won back a place in the affections of her schoolmates.

Fortunately, in Margaret's real-life situation, Miss Prescott showed the same common sense and compassion as Mariana's benefactor and helped her over the time of crisis. Without a doubt the experience left scars that never disappeared; but it also produced a new humility to counterbalance the fierce pride over which Margaret exercised precarious control. It led her also, as she wrote some years later, to dedicate herself to "the love of Truth and Honor." In the years that they knew her, Emerson, Alcott, and Theodore Parker all attested her success in keeping her pledge.

II Self-culture

Spurred on by ambition and a moral sense still accented by Puritanism, Margaret returned home from Groton to a strenuous campaign of self-culture. A typical schedule began a little before five in the morning and ended with the day's record in her journal shortly before midnight. In between she sandwiched singing, playing, and long sessions of studying philosophy and Italian and French literature. These activities came early in the day or in the late afternoon and early evening hours because her mornings were taken up with the study of Greek at Mr. Perkins' school in Cambridgeport. Here she managed to impress school fellows like Oliver Wendell Holmes and Richard Henry Dana with her superior knowledge and sagacity. Holmes found classmate Harriet Fay, "the golden blonde," more of a treat for schoolboy eyes; but he also recalled that Margaret attracted attention by the sinuous movements of her "long, flexible neck" and by making her eyes look small as if she were constantly peering into the sun. A confirmed mimic, he poked fun at her high-pitched voice and her talk about reading "naw-vels." [9]

Margaret was not unaware of her faults. She felt deeply the lack of natural tact and polish, and she determined to rub off the rough edges of her character. No obstacles seemed too difficult to overcome. She looked for someone upon whom she could model herself and considered the relative merits of the "brilliant" de Staël or the "useful" Edgeworth. Brilliance won out easily over practicality. She romanticized everything about her, found interesting parallels between Byron and Rousseau in her reading, and wished that she might be living back in feudal times when men and women "worshipped nature, not as high-dressed and pampered, but as just risen from the bath." [10]

The home on Cherry Street had served its purpose well when the Fuller family was smaller and less prosperous, but the arrival of James Lloyd in 1826 and growing political success induced Timothy Fuller to move his family to Dana Hill near the Harvard Campus. Here old friendships were taken up again and new associations quickly formed. When she was only thirteen, Margaret had met Henry Hedge for the first time and had impressed him as being precocious. Henry, the son of "Old Brains," master of logic to generations of Harvard men, had just returned to Harvard from five years in Germany with George Bancroft.[11] Now he was finished at the College and a student in the divinity school. Once again he found in Margaret a willing listener. Through him she discovered Germany and also received the impetus needed to start her on a study of German literature.

Hedge's portrait of Margaret's physical appearance at this time reveals a young lady of vigorous health and florid complexion with a tendency to be somewhat overweight. Though possessed of no outstanding feature, her face attracted attention by its lack of repose and its promise of character. By no standard beautiful, Margaret nevertheless had dancing eyes, excellent teeth, and an abundance of blonde hair; she could hardly have been called plain. Still she judged herself more harshly than Hedge because she had already decided to be "bright and ugly."

Social graces were another matter that troubled her. Margaret's were still far from being superior. In the summer of 1826 when Timothy Fuller gave a ball at the house on Dana Hill in honor of his political idol, President John Quincy Adams, Margaret served as her father's hostess. She stood self-conscious and awkward as she greeted guests in a gown that had met with Timothy Fuller's approval. Badly cut, too tight, and of a pinkish shade, her dress only accentuated every rebellious ounce of extra weight. Bright conversation and flashing wit are difficult to sustain under such handicaps, and one of the guests decided to take Margaret in hand to see how she could make some improvement. Eliza Farrar was the wife of Harvard's noted professor of astronomy and English by birth. She was highly accomplished in the social world, invited Margaret into her home, and opened up avenues of experience of which Margaret was completely unaware. Under the older woman's tutelage, Margaret learned to temper the brusqueness of her manners and to accommodate herself to the shortcomings of others.

She met new friends; among these the beautiful Southerner Anna Barker made the deepest impression. Long after their friendship had begun, Margaret was moved to write in her journal a description of their relationship. She had been stimulated by the sight of a print of Madame Recamier in her boudoir, which had then turned her thoughts to de Staël's relationship with Recamier. "It is so true," she wrote, "that a woman may be in love with a woman, and a man with a man." This love, she continued, "is regulated by the same law as that of love between persons of different sexes; only it is purely intellectual and spiritual." [12] Such was the passion that Margaret and Anna acknowledged for each other, and there would be counterparts in Margaret's later relationships with close friends Caroline Sturgis and Sarah Clarke. Not at all uncommon in an age that spread *Weltschmertz* rather liberally, Margaret's romantic and often-times exaggerated statements of feeling should not be translated simply into today's psychoanalytic jargon. A modern diagnosis of latent homosexuality explains no more than giving Plato credit for having taken all passion out of loving—and is far more likely to give rise to inferences that can not be supported.

Margaret was capable of falling in love in the heterosexual manner. As he made his way through Harvard with the class of 1829, George Davis, a distant cousin of Margaret's, had become a favorite of the Fuller family, spending many of his free hours at the house on Dana Hill and entertaining the entire family with his gay quips and ready smiles. Margaret felt more than a casual affection for this engaging youth; but he departed from the Harvard Law School with more serious thoughts on his mind than love, and she was left with an empty place in her heart to fill.

Recovery came much faster than she had expected. There were always studies in which to bury herself and new friends to bring her out of herself when the charm had departed from books. Two such youths were William Henry Channing and James Freeman Clarke, also members of that class of 1829 whose memory its poet laureate, Oliver Wendell Holmes, was to keep ever green. Margaret did not come to know Channing really well until some ten years later, but she called Clarke "cousin" and saw him nearly every day until she moved from Cambridge. Clarke's affection and regard for the "great soul" that he tried to immortalize in the *Memoirs* are a matter of record, but the publication of his correspondence with her over a period of nearly twenty years brings out facets of their relationship that Clarke hesitated to reveal in his public tribute.[13]

It seems quite clear that each depended upon the other to keep private confidences. James did not hesitate to regale Margaret with his numerous affairs of the heart; and Margaret, on one occasion at least, felt no compunction in frustrating a budding romance with her friend Elizabeth Randall. From the beginning Margaret and James were examples of the rule that opposites attract. Clarke especially felt the difference in the quality of their minds. "You in your worst estate," he wrote, "can think, and learn, and do more things than I in my best."[14] As they rode together on horseback between Cambridge and Newton or strolled beneath the lindens or in the garden of her home, they talked over plans for the future. By now, Margaret was convinced that conversation was her natural element. Despite efforts to write poetry and romances, she knew that her writing was "mighty dead." Writers, she told Clarke, seemed like pale shades by comparison with her "dear old Greeks, who talked everything." Because she recognized an element of dependence in her need to have others draw her out, she considered her mind "second-rate"; but Clarke told her that she was too self-critical and reminded her of the motto, "Extraordinary, generous seeking," which she had written in an album that she had given him.

Margaret was now twenty-one. Although fully aware of her unusual intellectual gifts and pleased by the admiration they elicited from friends, she felt restless and discontented. She entertained vague, formless fears of never being loved and of being set apart as a victim of the world's iron laws. For several years past, she had followed a code in which purity and harmony of character constituted the chief goals. She believed in a God of Beauty and Perfection, who appealed to her more on aesthetic than religious grounds; but she rejected particular revelations and creeds and disdained the refuge or protection of any institutional form of religion. Stoic and Roman in theory, she found in practice, however, that passion had a way of breaking through purely intellectual barriers. Conflict grew within her and intensified her restlessness. She became depressed and so convinced of the futility of mere intellect that she was tempted to throw aside everything that she was doing.

The crisis came on Thanksgiving Day. As she sat in church in compliance with her father's wishes and thought silently about her problems, she waited impatiently for the service to end. When it was finished, she walked rapidly away over the fields toward home. The emptiness within her was echoed by a universe from which all life seemed to have vanished. A cold blue sky looked down upon the dull hues of late autumn, and moaning gusts of wind played fitful counterpoint to the desolation of the season. Suddenly the sun came out. Like Thomas Hardy, leaning on his coppice gate and listening to the carolings of a darkling thrush at century's end, Margaret grew warm with new-found hope. Faith was at that moment reborn within her. She recorded the transformation in her journal when she returned home hours later beneath the rising moon: "I saw there was no self; that selfishness was all folly, and the result of circumstance; that it was only because I thought self real that I suffered; that I had only to live in the idea of the All, and all was mine. This truth came to me, and I received it unhesitatingly; so that I was for that hour taken up into God." [15]

How often in New England had such scenes been re-enacted! In similar fashion Jonathan Edwards had discovered the beauty of holiness, and William Ellery Channing had first beheld the glory of Divine disinterestedness while living on the very estate that Margaret Fuller had called home. Like these illustrious divines, Margaret was also to find a falling off from the heights of ecstasy; but she discovered, as had they, that failure and limitations were much more easily fitted into the context of living when one tempered self-love with altruism. She could now give devoted attention to Goethe's "extraordinary, generous seeking."

The following spring she began to study German. Both she and James Clarke had determined to learn the language when they were attracted by the "wild bugle-call" of Thomas Carlyle in the articles on Richter, Schiller, and Goethe that were appearing in the English quarterly magazines. According to Clarke, Margaret could read German with ease in three months. Before the year was done, she had read most of Goethe's better-known work, including *Faust, Iphigenie im Aulis, Tasso,* and had laid plans to translate the last-named work. In addition, she read Körner, Novalis, and Richter. For a time—but only briefly—she was seduced from Goethe by the beauties of Schiller's lyrics, which seemed so much warmer to her than Goethe's cold and "merciless" art. During this time she also read Schiller's principal plays.

At day's end, when she was surfeited with study, Clarke would come to visit; and the two of them would compare notes on their reading. James was almost as adept at translation as she and could hold her to standards as rigid as those by which she judged him. As they conversed and tested their ideas on each other, Clarke found Margaret coming back again and again to Goethe. Minds like Novalis appeared imperfect and "refreshingly human" to her, but Goethe impressed her as so immensely superior that he threatened to overwhelm her and steal from her the sense of personal identity. From this point on, Goethe became an agent of re-education, for through his eyes she learned to see a different world from the one that she had inherited from Puritan forebears.[16] After reading Goethe's "Second Residence in Rome," she wrote Clarke, "I shut the book each time with an earnest desire to live as he did,—always to have some engrossing object of pursuit. I sympathize deeply with a mind in that state. While mine is being used up by ounces, I wish pailfuls might be poured into it." [17]

III   *Rustication*

But Margaret's wish was not then to be realized. Her newborn humility and desire to be of service to others, however, were soon to be put to the test. Ever since Andrew Jackson had succeeded President Adams in the White House, the political fortunes of Timothy Fuller and other supporters of the National Republican party had been on the wane. Timothy had once dreamed of a foreign diplomatic post, but strong political activity on behalf of Adams not only precluded his sharing in the Democratic spoils system but also meant virtual political suicide. The mansion on Dana Hill, his symbol of political aspiration, had become forfeit in the fall of 1831. Then the family had moved into Uncle Abraham's home on Brattle Street to stay until Timothy could find a suitable farm to which he could retire, nurse his dyspepsia, and write his political memoirs. Although life under the roof of the stiff-necked Abraham Fuller had not always been pleasant, it was still a highly civilized existence. But it came to an end in the spring of 1833. The farm was located, and the Fuller family left Margaret's beloved Cambridge for Groton, the scene of earlier unhappy memories.

Groton was only forty miles from Boston, but the atmosphere of a small country town held no allure for a young woman accustomed to the stimulating intellectual and social existence of Cambridge. The omens had not been auspicious either; for upon her arrival, she found her ten-year-old brother Arthur crying for her and burning with fever from an accident that was later to cost him an eye. Work proved to be her salvation. Her mother became ill again and had to remain in bed much of the time. Grappling with the heavy chores of a country farmhouse and the busy routine of a large family used up much of Margaret's unusual store of nervous energy. But somehow she still found the strength to teach her sister Ellen and her brothers Arthur, Richard, and Lloyd when her father turned over the task to her so that he could get on with his book.

Although she always gave five, and sometimes eight, hours a day to instructing her pupils in languages, geography, and history, she managed to set aside time for herself for a course of study that included history, the elements of architecture, and the writings of Alfieri, Goethe, and Schiller. For the first time in some years, she found herself drawing closer to her father. As she read through Jefferson's letters, with him, she began to appreciate how fortunate the United States had been in its leaders. Timothy Fuller's knowledge and judgment of the founders of the Republic revealed to her a new side both of her father and of the great men whom he revered. Taking root were the patriotic fervor and the political liberalism that would one day result in heroic action during the days of the ill-fated Roman Republic.

The move to Groton meant separation from James Clarke and an end to their daily German sessions, but it also inaugurated a correspondence that continued for many years. Margaret sent Clarke her translation of Goethe's *Tasso*. After he had returned it with some criticisms of her metrics and encouragement to have it printed, she replied that she had little hope of seeing it published. She did, however, see her name before the public when the Boston *Daily Advertiser* printed, on November 27, 1834, her "Defense of Brutus," a rejoinder to George Bancroft's attack in the *North American Review*. Elation led her to write proudly to Henry Hedge, Bancroft's former charge, to tell him that she had even received a response to her article from "some big-wig" in Salem.[18]

Her triumph was really very small. Most of her writing projects proved too grandiose. Clarke, who was now a struggling young minister in Louisville, Kentucky, received word from her of plans for six historical tragedies and a series of tales about Hebrew history. For these "embryo designs," as she called them, she needed time and peace of mind, neither of which was likely to come her way while she was trying to fill the roles of mother, teacher, and student. Her most ambitious project concerned preparations for a life of Goethe, whose death two years before had inspired her to begin such a task. "Am I, can I make myself, fit to write an account of half a century of the existence of one of the master-spirits of this world?" she asked Clarke. And some-time later she wrote him, "I am shocked to perceive you think I am *writing* the life of Goethe. No, indeed! I shall need a great deal of preparation before I shall have it clear in my head." [19] Could she get information without going to Europe? she wondered. She thought of asking Carlyle for help but postponed taking any action.

Instead of forging ahead with her writing, she turned her attention to studying the evidences of Christianity. Plato's dia-logues still held their "enchantments" for her, but the *Phaedo* left many questions unanswered about the nature of Deity and the powers of the soul. The deism of some of her friends and her own scepticism also left her disquieted. She still looked, nevertheless, to Goethe for example, culling for her journal such thoughts of his as "Piety is not an *end* but a *means,* by which to attain, through the purest tranquillity of mind, the highest culture," and "In highest degree of perfection, the individual recognizes the *Divine in human nature* itself." [20]

At home her labors were beginning to lighten with the hiring of a servant. In June, shortly after her twenty-fifth birthday, she paid a ten days' visit to the Farrars in Cambridge, which acted upon her like a tonic. In great excitement she wrote her father for permission and money to accompany the Farrars and some friends to Trenton Falls in upstate New York. Timothy Fuller complied with all of his daughter's wishes, and she had one of the truly delightful experiences of her life in visiting Newport, West Point, and the falls at Trenton, the scene of Fanny Kemble's wooing and the setting for the lovers in Catherine Sedgwick's latest best-seller.

Much of her delight, if the truth be told, resulted from the companionship of the youthful Samuel Gray Ward.[21] Seven years her junior, Ward, who was to begin his senior year at Harvard in the fall, was inclined at first to be reserved in Margaret's presence because he had heard that she was a wit and a bluestocking. But Margaret's defenses melted before Sam's engaging smile, and she set herself to be her most ingratiating self. Art proved a common bond as well as literature. In almost everything, the college boy found in the older woman a store of learning wholly lacking in pedantry. To Margaret a new friend, especially one so attractive and so understanding, was indeed precious. With his picture in mind, she ended a sonnet composed on the journey with the line, "Since then no more alone at Nature's shrine I kneel."

Upon her return to Cambridge in the autumn, Margaret added another acquaintance. Harriet Martineau, the English authoress, whose *Illustrations of Political Economy* had caused her to be lionized in England, was completing a cross-country tour of the United States.[22] An ardent abolitionist, she had stirred up controversy wherever she traveled; but, as a guest of the Farrars, she proved a warm and engaging personality to whom Margaret was immediately attracted. She took pleasure in telling Miss Martineau about Dr. Channing, and both speculated upon what the good doctor would have to say in the pamphlet on slavery that was soon expected to be off the press. Among the earliest confidences that she had to share, Margaret talked of her desire to go abroad. She was overjoyed to be invited to join Miss Martineau and the Farrars when they sailed for England. The sailing was scheduled for the coming summer, and she would have time to win her father over to her side. After all, he had promised that he would pay her expenses as a reward for undertaking the education of the younger Fuller children.

The best of plans may never be realized. Shortly after returning to Groton, Margaret fell desperately ill and despaired of living. Undoubtedly, the major reasons for her illness lay back somewhere in the strenuous overwork of the previous two years. She was also constantly worried and upset by the thought that her mother might die. But the immediate cause of her becoming sick was the agony of guilt and embarrassment she felt upon learning that George Davis and Harriet Russell had been informed that she had made fiction out of their love affair. Margaret's story was entitled "Lost and Won." [23] Under rather thinly disguised names and incidents—according to James Clarke, who figured as the third party in *l'affaire* Davis and Russell—Margaret had tried to create an imaginative tale based upon the familiar triangular conflict between a ladylove and two adoring swains.[24] Nothing in this situation would stir the imagination, and that appears to have been the whole trouble. Margaret lacked the fictive power to transform actuality into literary reality; her zeal for truth had betrayed the artistic desire and had wounded her friends. She never tried her hand at fiction again, but the damage to her psyche could not be undone.

For nine days and nights, Margaret lay upon her bed in an agony of pain and fever. She suffered from a form of conversion hysteria, one might say today; but, nevertheless, her suffering was intense and real. Tended by her mother and watched over anxiously by her father, Margaret heard her father, for the first time in her life, speak with only tenderness in his voice: "My dear, I have been thinking of you in the night, and I cannot remember that you have any *faults*. You have defects, of course, as all mortals have, but I do not know that you have a single fault." [25] Timothy Fuller always tried to speak precisely. Even when he was breaking the habit of a lifetime to praise one of his children, he was careful not to use words loosely. They fell like a benediction, and it is more than probable that they had power to heal; for soon after Margaret began to recover.

Wherever one looks, there is irony in Margaret Fuller's life.

No sooner was she recovered and looking forward to the promise of a new relationship with the father whom she admired so much than he was taken sick. On the last day of September he was attacked by Asiatic cholera, and he died on October 1, 1835. The daughter in whom he had placed his highest hopes and from whom he had expected so much closed his eyes in death and drew the bereaved family about her. Then, upon her knees she vowed to keep faith with them and to see that they were protected.

CHAPTER 2

Giving Mind to the Public

"I am very ignorant of the management and value of property, and of practical details. I always hated the din of such affairs, and hoped to find a life-long refuge from them in the serene world of literature and the arts."—M.F.

TIMOTHY FULLER'S SUDDEN DEATH left his family totally unprepared. After Margaret had recovered sufficiently to think of practical concerns, she began to take stock of the Fuller fortunes. Since her father had made no will, Uncle Abraham Fuller had to be called to help settle the estate. A small income for Timothy's widow and the children—scarcely more than $500 a year for each—was all that could be expected, Uncle Abraham told her. When he advised against further schooling for the children, Margaret staunchly objected. She had no idea how she would manage, but she was resolved that Ellen and the boys would have all the education they needed.

Throughout the winter following Timothy Fuller's death, the family gradually began to piece together the broken pattern of their lives. Fighting hard against the necessity of giving up her visit to Europe, Margaret finally made her decision. She wrote rather wistfully to Sam Ward, who was accompanying the Farrars, that she could not go and asked for his continued friendship. On her birthday, she confided to her journal that she found little to console her in Goethe's *Lebensregel*, "enjoy the present and leave the future to God"; yet she was more determined to resist self and to act for others.

I *Looking About*

What could she do? She had little confidence in her writing ability, although she realized that sorrow and disappointment might easily account for her lack of faith in herself. When James Clarke had asked for her help the previous spring in filling the pages of his new periodical in Cincinnati, *The Western Messenger,* she had sent him articles on George Crabbe and Hannah More as well as pieces on Bulwer-Lytton and *Philip van Artevelde*.[1] Clarke, who had given her latitude to write on "religion, morals, literature, art, or anything *you* feel to be worth writing about," and who wrote, "Be as transcendental as you please," welcomed her contributions and printed them in the June, August, and December issues of the *Messenger*.[2] But he took her to task in his letters for faults of style and organization. People in the West, he told her, are practical and down to earth. They want ideas put straightforwardly in plain language without allusions and flowery language. They expect subjects to be fully developed and conversational in tone, though not quite so lofty as the one Margaret usually adopted.[3]

Since Clarke's criticisms were well founded, Margaret accepted them with good grace. As usual, she decided to study harder. "I have been examining myself with severity, intellectually as well as morally," she wrote Eliza Farrar, "and am shocked to find how vague and superficial is all my knowledge."[4] As she proceeded with her researches on Goethe, she discovered more and more areas of which she knew very little. She called upon Clarke to help her with some metaphysical inquiries, and he responded by identifying the differences he saw between the English and German schools of thought. Margaret asked him to define the term *transcendental*, and she got back Kant's answer that it referred, not to knowledge of objects themselves, but to "our means of knowing them, so far as they can be known, *a priori*."[5]

While she was reading at a rate that compared favorably with that of Gibbon—or so thought Ralph Waldo Emerson—Margaret finally realized her desire to become acquainted with that distinguished gentleman. As early as 1834, she had written Almira Barlow that Henry Hedge had spoken admiringly of "the Rev. W. Emerson, that only clergyman of all possible clergymen, who eludes my acquaintance. *Mais n'importe.* I keep his image bright before my mind." [6] A while later she urged Hedge to send Emerson her manuscript translation of *Tasso;* when she heard that Emerson had expressed interest in meeting her, she wrote back to Hedge: "I am flattered that Mr. Emerson should wish to know me. . . . I cannot think I should be disappointed in him as I have been in others to whom I had hoped to look up." [7] Several months later, they were finally introduced, probably at Mrs. Farrar's in Cambridge when Waldo and his brother Charles came to visit Harriet Martineau.

From that time on, Margaret left nothing to chance: she was really determined to know Emerson. After some maneuvering and letter exchanges, she was finally invited to Concord to spend three weeks with Emerson and his wife Lidian, who were still newlyweds learning to adjust to life together. The time was July, 1836.

It is difficult to know exactly all of Margaret's reasons for pursuing Emerson so doggedly, but one is certainly clear. She was looking for a guide—someone who could instruct her and show her a true vocation. In her journal, a short time before her visit, she copied down her hope that "some friend would do,—what none has ever yet done,—comprehend me wholly, mentally, and morally, and enable me better to comprehend myself." [8] Even if one allows for the degree of exaggeration to be found in soul-inventories in private journals, all the evidence points to the conclusion that Margaret Fuller had not yet found in the friendship of men like Clarke or Hedge, or in the companionship of the bright young women who so admired her, the strength and support that she needed to get outside herself and to free herself from what at times threatened to become a kind of sickly romanticism. Goethe still remained her chief literary guide, but he was not flesh and blood. She had heard Emerson preach, and his calm and unwavering approach to duty and his firm enunciation of principles led her to believe that she might find in him the guide for whom she had been searching. She was to discover that she was both right and wrong: Emerson undoubtedly helped to balance her enthusiasm, but he was not the kind of man to comprehend her wholly or, at times, even discern what she felt. Still their meeting was a fateful one with auguries of promising communion for both.

On Emerson's part, the visitor who stepped into his home and into his life on the twenty-first of July proved to be rather extra-ordinary. His first impression was unfavorable. Margaret had gone to some trouble to dress for the occasion, and Emerson was impressed by her ladylike self-possession; but her plainness and the nasal tone of her voice together with the trick of opening and closing her eyelids repelled him, and he said to himself, "We shall never get far." [9] He had not reckoned with Margaret's talents. Soon he found himself responding to the fun in her eyes and the drollery of her anecdotes; the initial physical impression was displaced by a completely new one in which the magnetism of Margaret's personality was recognized and given full justice. Her effect upon Emerson after little more than two weeks' acquaintance is summed up in a letter to his brother William, "It is always a great refreshment to see a very intelligent person. It is like being set in a large place. You stretch yourself and dilate to your utmost size." [10] Lidian Emerson's reaction was much more restrained but no less sincere: "We like her—she likes us," she told Elizabeth Peabody, who had taken a hand in bringing the Emersons and Margaret together.

At the Emersons, Margaret met various friends of the family, interesting persons to talk to—but none so unusual as Amos Bronson Alcott, who came to Concord for a day's visit on August 2. The talk of the group quickly centered around the Temple School that Alcott had founded two years previously and about Elizabeth Peabody's plans to leave the school for another under-taking. Margaret already knew something about Alcott's unique faith in the minds of children because she had read the *Record of a School,* the account of Alcott's conversations with his pupils published by Miss Peabody. When Alcott inquired whether Margaret would consider a teaching post, she withheld an immediate reply but promised to give him an answer soon. When she returned home, it did not take her long to decide. Her answer was yes.

II *The Temple School*

Autumn found her saying goodbye to her family and bidding farewell to the Wachusett and Peterborough hills, those twin symbols of aspiration that had helped to sustain her during the more than three years of her trials in the country. In Boston she rented rooms from her Uncle Henry, whose home at 2 Avon Place was within easy walking distance of the Temple School. By nine o'clock each day she was in the classroom ready to begin a busy schedule of instruction in German, French, Italian, and Latin. When Alcott resumed his conversations, she added the duties of a reporter to those of language teaching.

Although she admired Alcott for his sincerity and devotion to principle, Margaret held serious reservations about his almost complete reliance on intuition and his tendency to neglect experience. In her journal, she set down these feelings about the "Gospel of the Nineteenth Century" in an imaginary dialogue between Alcott and herself. After deciding that Alcott lacked a proper understanding of the nature of genius and of the reaction of matter on spirit, she concluded that his impatience with multiplicity was responsible for his often becoming lost in abstractions.[11] Alcott, on the other hand, had only the highest praise for his co-worker. "She takes large and generous views of all subjects, and her disposition is singularly catholic. . . . I think her the most brilliant talker of the day."[12]

Under ordinary circumstances, Margaret's heavy work load would not have daunted her. She even advertised for private students in foreign languages in October and asked Emerson to inquire at Harvard about the availability to her students of Mr. Sales and Mr. Bachi of the language staff for instruction in conversational French and Italian.[13] As if this was not already too much, she spent one evening a week at Dr. Channing's, translating De Wette and Herder with him, a rather slow process because Channing was not of a mind to keep up with her habit of "ducking, diving, or flying for truth."[14] Eventually the accumulation of work proved too heavy, and she became physically ill. Illness in turn brought on depression characterized by a romantic conception that somehow illness contributed to her being more creative. Like Thomas Mann, she was convinced— and remained so to the end of her life—that her mental powers expanded beneath the scourge of pain.

When April brought returning spring, she was beginning to think in a more healthful vein. "I have learned much and thought little," she wrote Henry Hedge. "I faint with desire to think and surely shall, the first opportunity, but some outward requisition is ever knocking at the door of my mind and I am as ill placed as regards a chance to think as a haberdasher's prentice or the President of Harvard University . . . I have been very unwell all winter and am now rather worse. . . . But I intend to get perfectly well, if possible, for Mr. Carlyle says, 'it is wicked to be sick.' " [15]

While she was debating how to secure more advantageous conditions for thinking as well as time to write her life of Goethe—she had never ceased to plan and gather materials but never seemed to reach the stage of actual composition—forces beyond her control were moving to close the Temple School and put her out of work. Early in 1837 the publication of the *Record of Conversations on the Gospels,* which Andrews Norton of the Harvard Divinity School labeled absurd, blasphemous, and obscene, brought down upon Alcott the criticism of Boston newspapers and the wrath of angry parents, who lost no time in withdrawing their youngsters from Alcott's care. No one wanted to hear Alcott's side of the matter, and Emerson was one of the few whose confidence in Alcott remained unshaken.

Even Henry Hedge was inclined to put Alcott in the pillory. When Margaret heard of Hedge's intentions, she wrote him asking, "Why is it that I hear you are writing a piece to 'cut up' Mr. Alcott?" Admitting that Alcott's system was not perfect, she told Hedge that he could perform a real service both to Alcott and to the public by writing an article that would reveal both its virtues and defects. "The phrase 'cutting up' alarms me," she continued. "If you were here I am sure that you would feel as I do, and that your wit would never lend its patronage to the ugly blinking owls, who are now hooting from their snug tenements . . . at this star of purest ray serene." [16]

III *Lady Superior in Providence*

Alcott intended to stick to his post as long as there was a single student, but he no longer needed an assistant. Margaret was jobless, and the prospect was not entirely displeasing. She needed a rest and a change of scene. She wrote Emerson, "I look to Concord as my Lethe and Eunöe after this purgatory of distracting, petty tasks. I am sure you will purify and strengthen me to enter the Paradise of thought once more." [17] Elysium in Concord, however, was not to be her portion for very long. She received an offer to teach at the Greene Street School in Providence, Rhode Island, at a salary of a thousand dollars a year—far more than Alcott had been able to pay her—for a teaching load much less demanding than that of the Temple School.

Although she disliked the idea of leaving Boston and her friends, particularly since she had received reports that Providence was a kind of cultural desert by comparison with Boston and also because George Ripley had just made her a fine offer to write a life of Goethe for his new series on foreign literature, the opportunity was too good to let pass. It would enable her to give her family more assistance, and it would provide her with the precious time for which she had long been wishing.

After a brief visit to Groton, she left for Providence in June, 1837, to take up her duties in the Greek temple that housed the new school of Hiram Fuller, an ambitious young man (but no kin to Margaret's branch of the Fuller clan) whose devotion to the teacher's calling was in direct proportion to what it could do to help him up fortune's ladder. Margaret's fears concerning the cultural climate of Providence were not totally unfounded. She discovered, as she told Alcott, "the element of money—getting with but little counterpoise." [18] When Emerson came to Providence on June 10 to dedicate the school, his audience showed little appreciation; and the Providence *Journal*, reporting on his address, labeled his remarks "so transcendental they were scarcely intelligible." Providence was too firmly anchored to the world of things to be carried away by mere idealism. It would need, Margaret decided, considerable cultural leavening before men like Alcott or Emerson would receive either understanding or acceptance.

Her teaching load turned out to be heavier than she had anticipated. The school of which she considered herself the "Lady Superior"—perhaps by way of identifying with one of her favorites in Germany, the Canoness Gunderode—contained nearly one hundred and fifty pupils; and, although she had been hired to supervise the elder girls, she soon found herself teaching boys as well as girls, and younger girls as well as the more advanced young ladies. The gulf between teacher and students exceeded even her most pessimistic forecast. Five or six years at the least, she estimated, would be necessary to make any real progress. The challenge was enticing, for she had been given complete freedom to try her own ideas. They were different ideas, she knew, for she was fully aware of how much her philosophy of education had been influenced by Bronson Alcott. "General activity of mind, accuracy in processes, constant looking for principles, and search after the good and the beautiful"—these were her goals; and every one of them would have merited the approval of the Socrates of Boston.

Upon her arrival in Providence, sickness had continued to plague her, but by July she was able to write Emerson that she had been enjoying good health for several weeks.[19] Once she felt like herself and after she had her classes under control, she began to take notice of the social scene about her. Despite Hiram Fuller's objections, she attended a Whig caucus, where she heard "the old bald Eagle," Tristram Burgess, indulge in tricks of oratory. "It is rather the best thing I have done," she wrote. "I now begin really to feel myself a citizen of the world."[20] She was badly disappointed in the lecture of Joseph Gurney, a celebrated English Quaker, especially since she had been more than once attracted by the doctrines of Quakerism. "One could not but pity his notions of the Holy Ghost, and his bat-like fear of light," she later reported. "His Man-God seemed to be the keeper of a mad-house, rather than the informing Spirit of all spirits."[21]

In order to enrich the program of her students, she invited lecturers from outside to address her classes. Richard Henry Dana, the father of her former classmate, lectured to them on the English dramatists, beginning with Shakespeare. Though she admired Dana's purity of taste and grace of manner, Margaret believed that he undervalued "the cannon-blasts and rockets which are needed to rouse the attention of the vulgar." The novelist and poet John Neal, a Yankee adventurer and a man of many parts, left quite a different impression. When he addressed her girls on the vocation of women in America, she found much in his remarks to disagree with; but his eloquence and brilliance, together with a certain sort of animal magnetism, affected her so deeply that she found herself wishing that she could share more of his company. Some of his ideas, too, undoubtedly remained in her memory to be dealt with at another time when she could voice her own sentiments regarding the place of women in American life.

By July, Margaret began to feel that her instruction was showing progress. "My plan grows quietly and easily in my mind," she wrote Elizabeth Peabody; "this experience here will be useful to me, if not to Providence, for I am bringing my opinions to the test."[22] Yet insecurity still gnawed at her peace of mind. On one such occasion she voiced her fears to Emerson. He responded rather oracularly with remarks he evidently thought so well of that he recopied and polished them for his journal and later incorporated some into his essay on "Self-Reliance." After reminding Margaret that "Power and Aim, the two halves of felicity seldomest meet," Emerson urged her to find an object worthy of her mind, some work that would be commensurate with her faculties. Failing that, she should remember that "Ethics . . . remain when experience and prudence have nothing to show. To feel and be heroic, is surely doing something, and is putting the capital of our being at rent in a bank that can not break, though its ostensible dividends may be far reversions. So let us deal justly, walk humbly, and all the catechism." [23]

The coolness of tone and lack of heart throb in Emerson's words awakened no fervor in Margaret's breast. There was too much "wild rush and leap, blind force for the sake of force" in her to accept "all the catechism." "Every year I live, I dislike routine more and more," she confessed, "though I see that society rests on that, and other falsehoods. The more I screw myself down to hours, the more I become expert at giving out thought and life in regulated rations,—the more I weary of this world, and long to move upon the wing, without props and sedan chairs." [24]

So she left Emerson to his own complacency for a while. But not for long. How could she fail to accept his urging to be self-reliant? When James Clarke questioned her about Emerson's preaching, she told him Emerson's influence was more beneficial to her than that of any other American. He taught me "what is meant by an inward life. Many other springs have since fed the stream of living waters, but he first opened the fountain. That the 'mind is its own place,' was a dead phrase to me, till he cast light upon my mind." [25]

She was still convinced that society was the source of evil, although she rejected any ideas of special providence and held the individual strictly accountable to his best genius. Thus Emerson's text—"Oh *my friends*, there are no friends"—seemed to her "a paralyzing conviction." [26] She could not accept his judgment and wished to visit her "dear *no friends*, Mr. and Mrs. Emerson" during her vacation.

On the last day of August, 1837, she was one of the audience who heard Emerson's address *The American Scholar* at the Phi Beta Kappa exercises. The sentiments, while certainly not new because Emerson had already read his *Nature* aloud to her and she was thoroughly familiar by now with his central doctrines of self-trust and self-realization, nevertheless filled her with pride. She even felt a thrill of self-accomplishment because she heard echoes of some remarks she had made to Emerson about Goethe. The necessity of the scholar to act, for instance. Perhaps those half-dozen lessons in German that she had forced on Emerson back in May had not been entirely wasted after all.[27]

After the exercises were finished, Margaret drove to Concord with the Emersons. The next day she attended a meeting at his home of the Transcendental Club. It was a rare occasion; for, besides Margaret, the women in Emerson's family—Elizabeth Hoar, Sarah Ripley, and Lidian—had been invited to join the ranks of a group that had formerly restricted its membership to males. At this meeting were fourteen men, among whom—in addition to Emerson himself—were Henry Hedge, George Ripley, and George Putnam. This was the original quartet of Unitarian ministers who had gathered after the bicentennial at Harvard in the autumn of 1836 to see what might be done to combat the suffocation overtaking the churches. From this beginning had stemmed the growth of what was sometimes called the Symposium or Hedge's Club since meetings were always called whenever Henry Hedge paid a visit from his parsonage in Bangor. Back in September, 1836, the first organizational meeting had been held at George Ripley's. Bronson Alcott, James Clarke, and Convers Francis had joined the group then; subsequent meetings at Emerson's, Dr. Francis' in Watertown, and Dr. Bartol's in Boston had drawn Theodore Parker, Orestes Brownson, John Dwight, and others of like mind.

A remarkable group: one could not find its like in America now or at any other time. No two thought alike; no two approached reality by the same route. Alcott's mysticism was offset by Brownson's radical reforming ideas; the solid scholarship of a Theodore Parker gave contrast to John Dwight's artistic flair, while Emerson and Ripley differed widely on how to improve society. *Mais n'importe,* as Margaret would say. What really counted was the amount of life in these men. Outsiders might make fun of what they considered a strange divorce of the practical from the ideal; they only showed their lack of comprehension of the revolutionary currents that rippled beneath the surface of "transcendentalism."

No one really knew what the name stood for. Margaret herself was a witness to that. Shortly after her entry into the group, she wrote, in response to an inquiry by Caroline Sturgis, this rather testy reply:

> *As to transcendentalism and the nonsense which is talked by so many about it—I do not know what is meant. For myself I should say that if it is meant that I have an active mind, frequently busy with large topics I hope it is so—If it is meant that I am honored by the friendship of such men as Mr. Emerson, Mr. Ripley, or Mr. Alcott, I hope it is so—But if it is meant that I cherish any opinions which interfere with domestic duties, cheerful courage and judgement in the practical affairs of life, I challenge any or all in the little world which knows me to prove any such deficiency from any acts of mine since I came to woman's estate.*[28]

When school reopened in September, Margaret returned to Providence. She remained there for the next sixteen months with only occasional visits to Boston to interrupt her routine. Her conversational powers had been noised about, and now she was invited out into society. She made new friends: one, the romantic widow, Sarah Whitman, whose verses appeared in the *Ladies Magazine* under the name of Helen (in later years the fiancée of Edgar Allan Poe); another, Anne Lynch, whose *soirées* for the New York "Literati" were still events for the future. On a much different plane was Margaret's friendship with a recent graduate of Brown University. Charles Newcomb was a would-be poet; ten years Margaret's junior, he possessed a somewhat feminine temperament coupled with a highly intuitive mind. This combination was well nigh irresistible to a woman of Margaret's sensibility, and she willingly assumed the role of priestess to her youthful votary. She gave him encouragement for his muse, and he reciprocated by acknowledging her as the one who had opened a new world for him.[29]

This was the world of music and art. During her visits to Boston, she took advantage of every opportunity to attend concerts and the theater and to view the art exhibits in the Athenaeum. As befitting what she called "an age of consciousness," music seemed to her "to contain everything in nature, unfolded into perfect harmony."[30] Mozart and Haydn were favorites, but Beethoven gave her the greatest pleasure. She saw Fanny Kemble perform in *Much Ado About Nothing* and came away disappointed; but of her performance in *The Stranger*, she wrote,

"That is genius. . . . I should like to recall her every tone and look." [31] This wish recalled a remark she had made to Emerson, "Who would be a goody that could be a genius?" [32] Truly, only genius mattered: it was both "poetry" and "religion," Emerson and she agreed, after watching a performance of the celebrated ballet artist Fanny Elssler.

Although music had power to evoke the strongest emotions in her, Margaret devoted a greater share of her Boston visits to architecture and painting. Sam Ward was back from Europe with his own paintings and many other treasures, and the interest in art that his letters from abroad had kindled could now be satisfied in his company. Raffaello, as she dubbed him, still had power to touch her emotions; he was the only one, she felt, who understood her at once in every mood. But he had already given his heart to Anna Barker. Margaret was keenly disappointed and hurt, but she found refuge from the "agonizing conflict of mind" in the Athenaeum, where Sam still acted as a faithful guide.[33]

Since 1823 the Athenaeum had housed an assortment of plaster casts selected by Canova, and now in 1838 its collection had been augmented by a costly series of engravings and drawings by Italian and French masters donated by the Brimmer family. Sam Ward himself had brought home from Italy several hundred designs of Raphael which he put in Margaret's hands. These riches were food for her soul. "How pure, how immortal, the language of form!" she exclaimed. "Who that has a soul for beauty, does not feel the need of creating, and that the power of creation alone can satisfy the spirit." To her, the artist seemed to be the only fortunate one; and she cried aloud, "Had I but as much creative genius as I have apprehensiveness!" [34] She was beginning now to form the patterns of taste that would characterize her approach to the arts throughout the rest of her life. Almost purely personal, her reactions were direct and emotional; they seldom reflected the artist's purpose but generally revealed not only her failure to build objective criteria but also her inexperience with the originals of great works of art. She dared to pass judgment after having looked at colorless prints and reproductions.

Critical as she was by nature, she was not content to be passive where creative energy was needed. She wrote an account of Karl Theodor Körner, the German poet and apostle of freedom, which appeared in two parts in the January and February, 1838, issues

of Clarke's *Western Messenger.* In May she was gratified to
receive Emerson's praise of her "Letters from Palmyra," which
had been published in the April issue. Superior tone, discrimination, lofty thought! These were Emerson's words and he prophesied "higher service" for her "golden pen." [35] James Clarke was
not so generous. "I should like to see a little more of *argument*
in your style," he wrote.[36] Emerson, too, after looking over a
portfolio of journals, letters, and poems that Margaret had left
with him, found a lack of abstract propositions. "If I write too
many aphorisms I think you write too few," he declared.[37]

What time she could spare from teaching, she gave to her
translation of Eckermann's *Conversations with Goethe.* Although
the work progressed and she salved her conscience for not getting
on with the biography of Goethe, her old enemy, ill health,
finally caught up with her. She had already begun to lose interest
in Providence because she missed her friends, especially Emerson; and she had found no one from whom to "kindle my torch
again. . . . And I see no divine person. I myself am more divine
than any I see. I think that is enough to say about them." What
really bothered her—and her physical ill-being only aggravated
the feeling—was that she had decided she could not serve two
masters. Teaching and writing just did not go together. "Isolation
is necessary to me, as to others," she told Emerson. She asked
him to send her his lectures on "Holiness" and "Heroism," but in
her heart she knew they carried no balm for her wounded spirit.[38]

She announced to Hiram Fuller that she was resigning her
post, and in December she bade her pupils farewell. It was a
sad occasion because mutual esteem had grown up between
teacher and students even though she had been, by all standards,
strict in discipline and objective in judgment, neither palliating
faults nor exaggerating virtues.[39] Teaching had been a valuable
experience, although she wrote her friend Almira Barlow: "I am
wearied out and I have gabbled and simpered and given my
mind to the public view these two years back, till there seems to
be no good left in me." [40] She never wanted to teach again, she
told William H. Channing. "If I consult my own wishes I shall
employ the remainder of my life in quite a different manner." [41]
So without any plans for the immediate future, she returned to
her family in Groton. The farm had been sold, but her mother
did not plan to move until April. There would be three blessed
months of rest and "Elysian peace."

CHAPTER 3

Transcendental Radical

"The primal duties shine aloft, like stars;
the charities that soothe, and heal, and
bless, are scattered at the feet of man,
like flowers."
—"Quoted from my beloved teacher
Wordsworth"—M.F.

WHEN BOSTON NEWSBOYS delivered the *Daily Advertiser* for August 27, 1838, containing Andrews Norton's
article, "The New School in Literature and Religion," they must
have found the paper hot to handle; for Norton, who fancied
himself a defender of public morality, had so forgotten decorum
as to lash out in rage, in the pages of a public newspaper, at
the most recent form of what he preferred to call "infidelity."
The immediate target of his spleen was the now-famous Divinity
School address delivered by Emerson on July 15 to the students
of divinity at Harvard; but Emerson's rebuke to the age, according to Norton, was only the culmination of a whole series of
subversive teachings that "is keeping our community in a perpetual stir."

Strewing epithets like "pantheist" and "hyper-Germanized"
among his charges, Norton went on to describe a "strange state
of things . . . in the literary and religious world" caused by the
growth of a new school that owes "its origin in part to ill understood notions, obtained by blundering through the crabbed and
disgusting obscurity of some of the worst German speculatists,
which notions, however, have been received by most of its disciples at second hand, through an interpreter." [1] The new school
was, of course, Transcendentalism; and its adherents were by no
means strangers to Margaret Fuller. Though she had told Henry

Hedge, as early as 1835, that she was merely "Germanico, and not transcendental," and had later qualified her position carefully for the benefit of Caroline Sturgis, she was the friend and confidante of James Clarke, Hedge, Alcott, and Emerson, who were now the leading spirits of the new ferment that aroused so much distaste in the Reverend Andrews Norton and other guardians of orthodoxy.

Norton's attack did not surprise Margaret, nor did she attach any weight to his strictures. She knew only too well the difficulties she had encountered in trying to penetrate the outer defenses of German philosophy, but she knew also that she had not been content to receive her notions "through an interpreter." When Carlyle had first aroused her interest in German studies, she had turned to Professor Charles Follen at Harvard for aid, and he had helped to temper her enthusiasm by insisting on first principles.[2] So she had read Locke, and then de Staël on Locke, before proceeding to Kant and the post-Kantians. All this was in preparation for her reading and study of Lessing, Schiller, Novalis, and Goethe. When she tried to read Fichte and Jacobi, she could figure out details, as we have seen, but systems eluded her. Even her reading of Buhle's and Tennemann's histories and her dipping into Scottish common-sense philosophers like Brown and Stewart provided little help. She translated De Wette and Herder and read Eichhorn and Jahn, but technical theology left no lasting impression on her mind.

So while it is true that interpreters like Carlyle and Coleridge exercised considerable influence upon Margaret's attitude toward the "spiritual philosophy" of Germany, she made heroic efforts to come by metaphysics at first hand. Although she failed, for she was simply not cut out to be a philosopher, she possessed the state of mind necessary to appreciate the tenets of transcendentalism without, at the same time, having a thorough understanding of their metaphysical foundations. Intuitions, which formed the basis for a large share of her beliefs, were often communicated to her in flashes of mystical insight during moments of near ecstasy. She never doubted them. Perhaps that is why she once said, "I now know all the people worth knowing in America, and I find no intellect comparable to my own."[3]

Beneath her thinking, then, lay the rich tradition of German idealism that permeated her reading in European authors from the early 1830's until she left for New York in the mid-1840's.

Though never systematically stated, her cosmology envisaged a universe in process—a state of becoming in which there were gradations ranging from nature through man to spirit. She believed strongly in an organic unity which pervades the fabric of being and stressed the interdependence of all parts of the world system. "Man," she declared, "is a being of two-fold relations, to nature beneath and intelligences above him. The earth is his school, if not his birthplace; God his object; life and thought his means of interpreting nature and aspiring to God." [4]

Since she viewed man's duty as that of an interpreter of nature, she found her own way to serve by acting as the medium through which the philosophy of idealism emanating from Germany could be grafted on to the native stock.[5] For, like Emerson, with whom she shared essentially the same metaphysical presuppositions, she was fully aware that a strong current of idealism had always run through American life. As Emerson tried to make clear in his lecture on transcendentalism in 1842, "the first thing we have to say respecting what are called *new views* here in New England, at the present time, is, that they are not new, but the very oldest thoughts cast into the mold of these times." He then continued:

The Transcendentalist adopts the whole connection of spiritual doctrine. He believes in miracles, in the perpetual openness of the human mind to new influx of light and power; he believes in inspiration, and in ecstasy. . . .

This way of thinking, falling on Roman times, made stoic philosophers . . . on popish times, made protestants and ascetic monks . . . on prelatical times, made Puritans and Quakers; and falling on Unitarian and commercial times, makes the peculiar shades of Idealism which we know.[6]

But if idealism had never left the American scene, the tide of rational conservatism was certainly running full in the late 1830's in New England. After listening to a sermon on the "rational" exercise of will and watching the upturned faces, "with their look of unintelligent complacency," Margaret was driven to say, "this Unitarianism has had its place . . . the time seems now to have come for reinterpreting the old dogmas. For one I would now preach the Holy Ghost as zealously as they have been preaching Man, and faith instead of the understanding, and mysticism instead, etc." [7] These remarks, and many others like them, made plain that Margaret's fundamental striving was a religious one although her method of expressing her convictions was dependent upon literature and its forms rather than upon theology. Emerson, Thoreau, and Alcott were no different. Andrews Norton was no man's fool; he had not been blinded by the literary masks of the young men who were leaving the Unitarian fold, and he labeled their defection for what he knew it to be— infidelity!

During the years from 1839 to 1844, when Boston was the center of her existence, Margaret Fuller showed by word and deed that she rightfully enjoyed her position as "a peer of the realm" among the leading transcendentalists. In many ways, her dissent seemed more radical to her contemporaries than that of the others: first of all, because she was a woman and dissent appeared unbecoming to a member of the gentler sex; second, because she left no doubt in the minds of those who heard her that she heartily disapproved of the current state of affairs. Summing up her general attitude toward society and her reasons for sympathizing with the "Transcendental party" are these remarks which she wrote in 1840:

> Since the Revolution, there has been little, in the circumstances of this country, to call out the higher sentiments. The effect of continued prosperity is the same on nations as on individuals,—it leaves the nobler faculties undeveloped . . . the tendency of circumstances has been to make our people superficial, irreverent, and more anxious to get a living than to live mentally and morally. . . .
>
> New England is now old enough,—some there have leisure enough,—to look at all this, and the consequence is a violent reaction, in a small minority. . . . They see that political freedom does not necessarily produce liberality of mind, nor freedom in church institutions—vital religion; and, seeing that these changes cannot be wrought from without inwards they are trying to quicken the soul, that they may work from within outwards. . . .
>
> Their hope for man is grounded on his destiny as an immortal soul, and not as a mere comfort-loving inhabitant of earth, or as a subscriber to the social contract. . . . Man is not made for society, but society is made for man. No institution can be good which does not tend to improve the individual. In these principles I have confidence so profound, that I am not afraid to trust

those who hold them. . . . They acknowledge in the nature of man an arbiter for his deeds,—a standard transcending sense and time—and are, in my view, the true utilitarians.[8]

I *Marking Time*

During the winter following her return to Groton, Margaret was continually beset by ill health, although she did not allow illness to prevent her from "paying some attention to Mother and Ellen when sick and teaching Ellen and Richard two afternoons in the week."[9] Between January and March she wrote fifty letters to various correspondents; finished and revised her translation of Eckermann; undertook to go through a forty years' accumulation of her father's papers containing more than a thousand letters; and, as a general counterpoint to this activity, continued with a heavy schedule of reading that included Plato, Coleridge, Goethe, Ben Jonson, and others. At night when she fell into bed, she read herself to sleep with Marryat's novels or chapters out of Disraeli's *Vivian Grey*. Occasionally she varied her bedtime reading by perusing the debates in Congress.

She made one brief visit to Boston to hear Emerson lecture but missed him because he was indisposed by a sleepless night and did not appear. Upon her return home, she chided him impishly, "Lose a night's rest! as if an intellectual person ever had a night's rest." The visit was by no means a loss: she talked with Alcott, who now appeared to her to deserve the praise Emerson was always bestowing on him ("I will begin him again and read by faith awhile"); at the Athenaeum she looked over a book of studies from Salvator Rosa, which pleased her and gave her ideas for her journal; and by no means least of all, she finally had an interview with Washington Allston, who was "as beautiful as the town-criers have said" and who "flamed up into a galaxy of Platonism" as he talked about his art.[10] Emerson liked Allston, too, but he considered his pictures "Elysian" and "unreal." Like all the artists, literary and otherwise, that America had so far produced, he thought Allston lacked "nerve and dagger." Margaret decided to withhold criticism until she had better grounds for judgment.

She was willing, however, to give Emerson her view of Jones Very's criticism of *Hamlet*. The youthful critic was one of Emerson's problem young men: Waldo felt responsible for him, but he feared that Very was either dying or "becoming hopelessly mad." [11] Margaret had yet to meet Very, but his characterization of Hamlet made her eager to know this young poet, who saw in Shakespeare's tortured prince the embodiment of a romantic hero beset by the crass material world. Although she considered Very as a critic, "infinitely inferior in accuracy of perception to Mr. Dana" and lacking his insight, "he soars higher," she told Emerson. [12] That alone made him Dana's superior, in her philosophy.

On March eleventh, the Groton farm was finally sold. Margaret enlisted Emerson's help in hunting for a suitable house for the Fullers in Concord; he offered her a home in his castle until she found a place, but she finally rented a large house in Jamaica Plain near Willow Brook and conveniently close to Boston and Cambridge. Now she was able to take a more active part in the Transcendental Club. Plans were afoot that spring, according to the comments Alcott made in his diary, to start a journal for the purpose of "circulating the thoughts which are not talked about in private circles." [13] In May, the club discussed the current state of journalism, finding Brownson's *Boston Quarterly Review* sound but not up to the standard they wished for their new periodical. On the twenty-seventh of the month, the *Daily Advertiser* announced the publication of her translation of Eckermann's *Conversations*.

She felt shamelessly proud—her first published book. James Clarke wrote and complimented her: what he had to say about the clarity and cogency of the Preface was especially gratifying. Emerson also lauded the Preface as "a brilliant statement" both "for itself, and for its promise." She need have no worry, he told her, about writing further on Goethe. [14] Margaret herself knew how much more she had dreamed of doing; as a matter of fact, however, she deserved much credit for throwing light on little-known aspects of Goethe's later career. By taking up the cudgels in his defense against charges that he was not a Christian, or an Idealist, or a Democrat, or Schiller, she presented him in a more attractive guise to the younger transcendentalists like Thomas W. Higginson, who credited Margaret's little book with bringing him closer to Goethe than any other book had ever done. [15]

When summer came, Margaret began to think seriously about the next stage in her career. She had been lazy long enough—if one could call a life of study and writing lazy—and now she had to find a way to earn money. She talked matters over with James

Clarke's friend, the Reverend William H. Channing, who had just returned from Cincinnati and who had gradually begun to fill the place in her affections left empty by Clarke's absence and by Sam Ward's defection to Anna Barker. She also became better acquainted with Theodore Parker, whose church in West Roxbury was nearby. On one occasion when she had been visiting the "Gigman" world of Boston, she had been introduced to Parker at a party; but before she could direct the conversation to Spinoza, she had been carried off by her hostess. Now she could indulge herself in lengthy conversations, although Parker's prickly personality presented a challenge. If she had been able to read his journal, she might have been taken somewhat aback by the candor of his remarks. While he prized Margaret's critical powers, he concluded "she puts herself upon her genius rather too much." [16] He told Emerson that she reminded him more of Madame de Staël than any woman he had ever met.

II *The Conversations*

In the autumn of 1839 Margaret wrote a letter to Mrs. George Ripley which she hoped to have circulated among the ladies of Boston. In the letter she outlined her plans to have the well-educated and thinking women of the community gather for the purpose of ascertaining "what pursuits are best suited to us, in our time and state of society, and how we may make best use of our means for building up the life of thought upon the life of action." [17] This was the beginning of her famous Conversations, which she gave annually for the next five winters until her departure for New York. It was also the real beginning of her influence upon women who would, by precept and example, one day prove their right to be treated as equals by their men. In a sense, it was also a source of many of the ideas and conclusions that would receive written exposition in *Woman in the Nineteenth Century*.

The idea for the Conversations may have come from that same Madame de Staël to whom Theodore Parker thought Margaret bore such a resemblance. It might also have been suggested by the experience of Elizabeth Peabody, who had held conferences with groups of women in 1833 and 1836 and in whose parlor at 13 West Street, Boston, Margaret held her opening session on November 6, 1839. The first course consisted of thirteen meetings, each two hours long, which usually began at noon. In a daring effort to relate past and present, Margaret chose Greek mythology for her subject, using the forms of Grecian myth and fable to express symbolically the relations between the human constitution and nature. Thus Jupiter stood for Will; Mercury for Understanding; Bacchus, "the abandonment" of Genius; Venus, instinctive womanhood; and Diana, chastity.

Margaret's usual practice was to introduce the subject under discussion, throw out some leading ideas, and suggest directions in which further investigation might take place. Then she would wait for others to contribute their thoughts. At first, only ten or twelve in the group spoke up; under Margaret's persuasive urging and guidance, everyone gradually began to participate. Passive onlookers had no place in these meetings; Margaret had made this plain at the outset. She told Mrs. Ripley that she proposed to give women an opportunity "to systematize thought, and give a precision and clearness in which our sex are so deficient . . . because they have so few inducements to test and classify what they receive." [18] During the first meetings, when the conversation was less satisfying than she thought it should be, she asked the class to write out their thoughts. At the next meeting she read aloud these "skarts of pen and ink," which served very efficiently as thought-clarifiers. In time, she found this practice was no longer necessary.

So much interest was aroused by Margaret's first series that another was arranged for the following winter on the subject of Fine Arts. In 1839 and 1840, according to Emerson, Bostonians and their neighbors fell in love with the genius of Italy. "Our walls were hung with the prints of Sistine frescoes," he claimed; "we were all petty collectors; and prints of Corregio and Guercino took the place, for the time, of epics and philosophy." [19] In addition the sculptures of the native artists—Horatio Greenough, Thomas Crawford, and Hiram Powers—were exhibited in the Allston Gallery. Local enthusiasm ran high; Margaret's was especially so since Emerson reports that in the summer of 1840 she "underwent some change in the tone and direction of her thoughts . . . threatening to arrive presently at the shores and plunge into the sea of Buddhism and mystical trances." [20]

In the arts then Margaret found an outlet for her surcharged emotions, and never more effectively than when she sat among the group of ladies who attended her class, throwing out a hint here, elucidating an allusion there, always leading and encouraging members of the group to do their own thinking, but investing the capital of the group in ideas that provoked further enterprise between one class and those to follow. She found all the women in the group to be intelligent, and five or six had talent. [21]

Even by Margaret's exalted standards, it was a distinguished assembly of New England women. The three Bostons were well represented: The Brahmin intellectual, the merchant's wife, and the ardent reformer sat side by side and engaged one another in animated debate. Mrs. Josiah Quincy, the wife of a very proper Bostonian; Mrs. George Bancroft, wife of the historian, himself a believer in transcendental self-reliance and a supporter of the Democratic cause; the three Peabody sisters—Mary and Sophia, engaged to Horace Mann and Nathaniel Hawthorne, respectively, and Elizabeth, a worshiper of Dr. Channing and of Emerson as well; Maria White, no especial friend of Margaret's but devoted to abolition and to her fiancé, James Russell Lowell; Lydia Child, the well-known authoress and abolitionist; Theodore Parker's wife; and many other wives, sisters, and daughters of Boston's finest families attended the Conversations faithfully and came away fortified with purpose and with the training to change society and women's role in it.

Not everyone thought so highly of the group's purposes or of Margaret's leadership. Her erstwhile friend Harriet Martineau had been sorely tried the year before by Margaret's criticism of her book *Society in America*. It had required courage for Margaret to take issue with Miss Martineau; but love of truth and candor led her to question the Englishwoman's intemperance of expression, particularly as it related to her tirade against Bronson Alcott and to her defense of abolitionism. [22] Now, in retaliation, Harriet lashed out against "the gorgeous pedants," a self-elected group who listened and discoursed "about the most fanciful and shallow conceits which the Transcendentalists of Boston took for philosophy" while "the liberties of the republic were running out as fast as they could go, at a breach which another sort of elect persons were devoting themselves to repair." [23] Events were to prove, of course, that Miss Martineau's distinction existed only in her imagination, for the two groups of "elect" were almost identical in personnel.

Despite criticism the Conversations continued to flourish. In

March, 1841, Margaret conducted an evening series for both men and women. The subject was Greek mythology as seen through art. At the ten meetings, attendance usually ran to about thirty, according to Catherine Healey Dall, one of the younger members of the group, who left a written record of her experiences many years later.[24] Hedge, Clark, Jones Very, William Wetmore Story, Bronson Alcott, George Ripley, and Charles Stearns Wheeler attended meetings faithfully, but Emerson attended only once because of the press of other engagements and his distance from Boston. The presence of the men served, on some occasions, to dampen the ardor of some of the women, but Margaret was no stranger to mixed intellectual company and carried on with her usual regal air. On the occasion of his only visit, Emerson, as seen through the eyes of a feminine participant, only served to display Margaret to advantage: "With his sturdy reiteration of his uncompromising idealism, his absolute denial of the fact of human nature, he gave her opportunity and excitement to unfold and illustrate her realism and acceptance of conditions." [25]

The following winter ethics provided the general theme of the Conversations. Daemonology, Creeds, the Ideal were taken up the next year, and in the winter of 1843 education was the general subject. No special effort was ever made to adhere rigidly to any kind of syllabus, and some of the most successful meetings resulted from diversions and extraneous topics introduced into the discussions by members who had ranged far afield in their studies. There was, however, a major emphasis that seldom disappeared from Margaret Fuller's leadership of the Conversations during the six years which she conducted them. This in essence was a moral emphasis. Her fundamental thesis was that all persons, regardless of race, sex or previous condition of freedom or servitude, carried moral freedom within themselves. Each man and woman, she believed, possessed a moral sense whose functions were to give direction and energy to the human will and to provide light and convincing evidence to the mind.

Unlike the French literary salons with which she was familiar and which had given women like Madame de Staël opportunity to display their brilliance and wit, Margaret's "parlatorio," as Emerson described it, became the setting for something more than a display of charm and talent: it was an arena in which women could learn about moral values and where they could, in

Hegelian fashion, strive for the ideal by pitting good against evil—where, in fine, they could learn that thought catches fire from a thinker, if one "be let loose upon the planet." [26] The life of "Poesy" (the Germanism Margaret borrowed from Goethe, Novalis, and Schelling to describe the heights and fulfillment of man) was "the ground of all the arts, and also of the true art of life; it being not merely truth, not merely good, but the beauty which integrates them both." [27] In their essence and aim, she counseled her women, the free poetic element and the spirit of religion are one, although "rarely in actual existence." Thus her already considerable interest in the arts became intensified because she saw them as vehicles for spiritual thought, and she wished others to share in the knowledge she considered so essential for sound living.

Although it is impossible to evaluate, in individual cases, the influence of Margaret's Conversations, their impact first of all upon the Boston community was considerable, and later upon the entire country, as evidenced by the testimony of Emerson and others who lived to see Margaret's teaching bear fruit in the establishment of women's study clubs, colleges for women, and conferences devoted to the cause of feminism. Upon Margaret herself they had also worked their influence. If anything, they had made her even more certain of her superiority and power over others. Humility in public still came as an after-thought: "God forbid that any one should conceive more highly of me than I myself," she declared, although in her private journal the tone of entreaty and prayer that she might become a better person is characteristic. The price of her public appearances before her women friends and students was frequently paid in fearsome headaches that fastened their hold of iron upon her even before she had reached home after the meetings had concluded. Her general mood for most of this period during which her reputation was spreading can be summed up by the comment that appeared in her journal shortly after she had given her last Conversation: "With the intellect I always have, always shall, overcome; but that is not half the work. The life, the life! O, my God! shall the life never be sweet?" [28]

III   *The Dial*

During the first winter that Margaret Fuller conducted her Conversations she was also busy preparing to inaugurate a new career as the editor of a representative journal which would express what was in the minds and hearts of thinking men. She had taken active part in the meeting of the Transcendental Club on September 18, 1839, when the decision to begin such a periodical was made; in November she had agreed to become its editor. Her letter to William Henry Channing on March 22, 1840, reveals the idealism of her project as well as the impossibility of its ever being realized by practical men working in an everyday materialistic world. "A perfectly free organ is to be offered for the expression of individual thought and character," she writes. "There are no party measures to be carried, no particular standard to be set up. . . . I hope . . . that this periodical will not aim at leading public opinion, but at stimulating each man to think for himself, to think more deeply and more nobly by letting them see how some minds are kept alive by a wise self-trust." [29]

Although not sanguine about obtaining talented writers for the new journal, Margaret was inexperienced enough to believe that contributors would work without pay. She was soon to discover how few such disinterested souls there were. By April, she was able to see more clearly some of the obstacles that lay ahead. "Things go on pretty well," she wrote, "but doubtless people will be disappointed, for they seem to be looking for the Gospel of Transcendentalism." She disparaged her own role as editor, telling William H. Channing, "I do not expect to be of much use except to urge on the laggards and scold the lukewarm and act like Helen McGregor to those who love compromise by doing my little best to sink them in the waters of oblivion." [30] Throughout the spring she wrote numerous letters to friends, soliciting poetry and prose contributions, and she almost single-handedly performed the work of an entire editorial staff. George Ripley was her business manager, and Emerson was her co-editor; but the bulk of the work and responsibility fell on her shoulders. The new journal was to be a quarterly appearing in January, April, July, and October, and each issue was to contain 136 octavo pages. By dint of almost herculean efforts, the first number was off the press on July 1, 1840.

From the first, *The Dial*, named according to Alcott after the title of his private journal, possessed a literary character in contrast to the historical stamp of the *North American Review* and the theological odor of the *Christian Examiner*, its predecessors on the New England scene. As Emerson stated in his address to the reader in the opening number—a reworking of Margaret's introduction but one of Emerson's most characteristic and felicitous utterances—the editors were not depending upon "the pens of practised writers." Not wishing "to multiply books, but to report life," *The Dial* was strictly an original, depending upon private diaries, unpublished poetry, and spontaneous criticism to fill its pages. Herein lay both its strength and weakness, more particularly perhaps during the first two years of its operation while Margaret was editor; for she took Emerson's address seriously and opened the pages of *The Dial* to those who might otherwise fall short of her standards both as critics and as writers as long as they qualified as free spirits earnestly thoughtful and sincerely desirous of communicating heartfelt sentiments to the world.

For her first issue Margaret had to rely for contributions upon her closest friends. Among the women of her circle, Sarah Clarke and Ellen Hooper offered short verses; from the group of men who had attended her Conversations, Dwight, Ward, Ripley, Cranch, and Alcott sent in selections; and she and Emerson filled up the remaining pages. Margaret's significant contributions were "A Short Essay on Critics," one of the most successful of all the efforts among the transcendentalists to define the critical mission of writers in a country attempting to establish a new literature, and her "Record of Impressions," a testimonial of her reactions to the Allston art exhibit of the previous summer. The rest of her offerings were poems of no particular value, although one, bearing the innocent title "A Dialogue," contains highly suggestive sexual imagery and involves a flower's invitation to be ravished by the sun god who, it might be added, finds no time from business to accept love's dalliance.

Looking at the first number in print, Margaret suffered because of its shortcomings. "I feel myself how far it is from the eaglet notion I wanted," she told Emerson.[31] He, in turn, had found several things to criticize about format, mostly matters of detail that surprised Margaret, who had not thought him so interested in mere externals; but in general he considered the July issue "a good book," which the public ought to accept as such.[32] Later, in August, he wrote that he would like to see a different *Dial*, one not "too purely literary." "I wish," he told Margaret, "that we might court some of the good fanatics and publish chapters on every head in the whole Art of Living." [33] Margaret certainly did not disagree; but she had her hands full, first with the task of securing material and then with seeing it through to publication; she was not about to debate the rationale for the next number while there was still question about filling out its pages.

Perhaps the best evidence of *The Dial's* vitality is the criticism it aroused. The Philadelphia *Gazette* called the editors, "Zanies" and "Bedlamites"; the New York *Knickerbocker* wrote amusing parodies of Alcott's "Orphic Sayings," perhaps the chief target for abuse in the entire history of the magazine; and even Emerson was criticized for his "literary euphuism." When Carlyle received the first number, he wrote Emerson: "Of course I read it with interest; it is an utterance of what is purest, youngest in the land; pure, ethereal, as the voices of the Morning! And yet—you know me—for me it is too ethereal, speculative, theoretic. . . ." [34] Later numbers impressed Carlyle more favorably, yet he continued to say that it needed more "body" to temper its greatness of soul.

The transcendentalists themselves found much to criticize. According to Sophia Ripley, who was in a position to view the editorial labors at close hand, "George, Margaret, and Theodore [Parker] all run it down unmercifully. It has not fire and flame enough for them. . . ." [35] Her husband's response to critics of the magazine is characteristic: "They expected hoofs and horns, while it proved as gentle as any sucking dove." Alcott called it a "twilight 'Dial' "; he felt that it allowed public opinion to overawe it, and he waited for it to become more original. Parker, on the other hand, said that it needed a beard; later on, according to Thomas Higginson, Parker's *Quarterly Review* succeeded in becoming the "beard without a 'Dial.' "

Editorial responsibilities at best are nerve-wracking, but Margaret Fuller worked under almost insuperable handicaps. Without much salary to speak of (she never received the entire amount of two hundred dollars a year she was promised); without funds to pay contributors, who then adopted a cavalier attitude toward deadlines; working with publishers who had money troubles of their own; and finding herself, again and again as publication dates approached, with space to be filled, Margaret needed all her resources to keep going. It required considerable tact and patience—qualities for which she had never been noted—to convince Alcott, for example, that *The Dial* was not simply a window to display his talents; or to woo bits of love verse from Parker, who held no illusions about his proficiency as "an amatory poet"; or to reject Henry Thoreau's essay on "The Service," and later one of his poems, without either offending or discouraging the young author.[36]

Despite these problems, Margaret carried out her responsibilities to the best of her ability. She was an impartial editor, fair but discriminating according to her own best standards; and she would not countenance slipshod work, although time has proved that much which more disciplined students of language and more objectively critical stylists would have rejected evaded her editorial glance. Emerson was one who did not escape what she called her "impertinence." She commented on particular phrasings in his article on modern literature, questioned his use and meaning of words, and even suggested that he had been trite. "I think when you look again," she wrote, "you will think you have not said what you meant to say." [37]

In many ways Margaret differed with the opinions and ideas of the leading spirits among the transcendentalists. For one thing, she was much less optimistic than many of her associates concerning any immediate revolution in the human condition. "Utopia," she said, "it is impossible to build up." [38] For another, she lacked the experiences that they as men had been able to enjoy so that her basis for judgment was more limited than theirs. But she never used her position as a woman as an excuse to escape her duty; and where matters of fundamental policy were involved, she was fearless in defending her point of view even when her opponent happened to be Emerson. Thus, she wrote him, after he had taken over the editorial chair from her, a carefully worded letter that reveals a significant difference in their ways of thinking.

As editor, she told Emerson, she had tried to produce a magazine that would suit more than one class of readers:

I thought it less important that everything in it should be excellent, than that it should represent with some fidelity the state of mind among us, as the name of 'Dial' said was its intent. . . .

You go on a different principle; you would have everything in it good according to your taste, which is, in my opinion, though admirable, as far as it goes, far too narrow in its range. . . .

I do not care for your *not liking* the piece, because when you wrote in your journal that I cared for talent as well as genius, I accepted the words written in dispraise as praise. I wish my tastes and sympathies more expansive than they are, instead of more severe. Here we differ.[39]

The eclecticism of taste that is voiced in these remarks was indeed characteristic of Margaret Fuller's editorial direction of *The Dial*, just as it was to be a guiding rule when she occupied a chair as literary editor on Horace Greeley's *Tribune*. Criticism should not "disparage and displace," she wrote in her journal, "but appreciate and classify what it finds existent." [40] So she recognized talent as well as genius, understanding as well as reason, but she believed in keeping each in its place.

She had no illusions where she herself stood as a writer. "It is very difficult to me to resolve on publishing any of my own writing," she told William H. Channing; "it never seems worth it, but the topmost bubble on my life. . . ." [41] Circumstances forced her, however, to use many of her own writings to piece out issues: she got out the October number in 1841, for example, only because eighty-five of the one hundred and thirty-six pages were filled with her own compositions; later, when she had resigned the editorship, she did what she could to help Emerson as a contributor. His testimony to her unselfishness, coming as it does from one who worked closely with her throughout the entire period of her editorship, is worth noting:

> She put so much heart into it that she bravely undertook to open, in the Dial, the subjects which most attracted her; and she treated in turn, Goethe and Beethoven, the Rhine and the Romaic Ballads, the Poems of John Sterling, and several pieces of sentiment which spared no labor; and, when the hard conditions of journalism held her to an inevitable day, she submitted to jeopardizing a long cherished subject, by treating it in the crude and forced article for the month.[42]

When Weeks and Jordan, the publishers of *The Dial*, failed in its second year of operation, and Margaret realized that it was futile to expect remuneration for her labors, she decided to give up the editorship. Her strength had been severely taxed to carry on both her Conversations and *The Dial*, and she knew she would be foolhardy to exhaust her resources even further. In

March she announced her intention to Emerson and asked for a prompt answer to her question whether he or Theodore Parker would carry on in her place. In spite of his better judgment, Emerson accepted the assignment, saying, "Let there be rotation in martyrdom"; and Elizabeth Peabody agreed to be his publisher, although even the indomitable Elizabeth must have gulped hard when she discovered that the subscription list numbered no more than three hundred names.

Immediately after relinquishing her post, Margaret went to Canton, Massachusetts, to visit one of her aunts and to recuperate for a few weeks. Another chapter in her life had closed, and the ending was not quite what she had hoped it might be. Though it is likely that she did not have serious regrets, it seems probable that she did not realize how much of a success she had been. It is more than evident from the testimony of Emerson and others who knew what she had done that *The Dial* would never have come into being or remained alive without her sacrifices and guiding hand. When the pages of the *Christian Examiner* were closed to the "infidel" party, she gave them a platform from which to express their ideas freely and fully. She goaded the lazy ones into utterance, and she rode herd on the more irrepressible spirits among them. Her wise policy of encouraging talent as well as genius may have evoked laughter and even scorn; but posterity is the benefactor, for she established the pattern in which the voice of New England could speak in authentic accents at a time when New Englanders had something revolutionary to say about the nature of man and the cosmos in which he dwelled.

IV *Brook Farm*

When the Reverend George Ripley wrote his remarkable letter of resignation on October 1, 1840, to his congregation on Purchase Street, Boston, he told his people that he was of that party which looked "forward to a more pure, more lovely, more divine state of society than was ever realized on earth." Although he also told them that he did not feel it his duty "to unite with any public association for the promotion of these ideas," [43] before the month was out he had talked with Margaret Fuller, Emerson, and Alcott about establishing a new community in the country. Alcott had ideas of his own which he later incorporated into his

Fruitlands; while Emerson, protesting that he had not yet "conquered" his present house, wrote in his journal, "I do not wish to remove from my present prison to a prison a little larger." [44] Margaret was interested but somewhat dubious. She had had her fill of farm life. Then, too, she saw certain inconsistencies in Ripley's views and thought he rushed into things before he had taken time to think them through. Although she would not dash cold water on his plans, she decided to do nothing except "look on and see the coral insects at work." [45]

While Ripley was formulating further plans, Margaret luxuriated in a three days' vacation with her friend Carrie Sturgis. As they sat before the wood fire in the evenings or rowed about on the river at Newbury during the glorious autumn days, she thought about the stir that was being made all around the New England countryside by reformers; and she whispered to herself, "I could frame my community far more naturally and rationally than Ripley." Then she let her imagination people the banks of the stream and the surrounding valleys with a "fair company," all living in harmony, thinking lofty thoughts and discussing "the high mysteries that Milton speaks of." An autumnal idyll, her dream grew out of the spell cast by the rich and productive land; like a thousand others, it overlooked the crags and depths of human nature. It was, moreover, a response to her distrust of ambitious social planning, although she had no doubt that "many persons will soon, somewhere, throw off a part, at least, of these terrible weights of the social contract, and see if they cannot lie more at ease in the lap of nature." [46]

In December, it seemed to her that Ripley was not likely to be one of these people. " 'Community' seems dwindling to a point," she wrote William H. Channing. "We are not ripe to reconstruct society yet." Later, at the end of March, she told him that she did not believe in society with a capital S. "I feel," she said, "that every man must struggle with these enormous ills, in some way, in every age. . . . So it has not moved me much to see my time so corrupt, but it would if I were in a false position." [47] Consequently, the spectacle of Ripley out surveying a possible site for his farm did not move her to high hopes.

But Ripley himself was not dismayed; for in April, 1841, he began in West Roxbury the experiment in social planning known as Brook Farm. Organized as a joint stock company, with shares of five hundred dollars apiece on public sale at Elizabeth Peabody's bookshop, the experiment attracted a small group of idealists—at first the Ripleys and a few close friends like John Sullivan Dwight, then later young men like Charles Dana and Nathaniel Hawthorne, who put all their savings in the new venture. As time went on, the numbers increased to include a broader base of membership, and through the influence of Albert Brisbane, one of the most ardent of the disciples of Charles Fourier, the community became more formally Fourieristic.[48]

Margaret never joined Brook Farm although she enrolled her sixteen-year-old brother Lloyd as a student. Lloyd was the last of the Fuller children and a slow learner with the refractory nature that sometimes accompanies dullness. Margaret knew in her heart that he could never qualify for college, but she hoped against hope that the atmosphere of Brook Farm might produce the miracle. Needless to say, it did not.

Keeping in touch with Lloyd provided one of her reasons for visiting "the fledglings of community," but there were others just as good. The Ripleys were close friends with whom she liked to converse; and she relished the rich talk of John Dwight and the Curtis brothers, who found her conversations equally worthwhile. Charles Newcomb was now a boarder at Brook Farm, and he had not lost his interest in Margaret. With his attraction to the symbolism and ritual of the Roman Catholic Church, he offered a sharp contrast to the other residents at the Farm, who viewed somewhat skeptically the pictures of Christian saints that covered the walls of his room in the "Eyrie." Margaret found herself once again responding to his moodiness, which was perhaps the necessary accompaniment to the "true genius" that Emerson found in Newcomb's writing in *The Dial*.[49] She thought how much Newcomb differed from Henry Thoreau, who rowed her about in the ponds near Concord and told her earnestly about his plans one day to be a farmer. Henry was as doubtful as she about solving society's problems in groups.

At the Farm, Margaret also became better acquainted with Nathaniel Hawthorne. When he first met Margaret, Hawthorne had shied away. He disliked on principle women who displayed their minds to the world and was somewhat suspicious of the influence Margaret might exert upon his fiancée, Sophia Peabody, who was a regular member of Margaret's conversation classes. On one occasion, when he received an invitation to dine at George Bancroft's home with Margaret present, he begged off and later wrote in his notebook: "Providence had given me some business to do, for which I was very thankful." [50] Although his shy and retiring nature continued to balk Margaret's efforts to penetrate his inner defenses, when Sophia wrote about her impending marriage, Margaret wrote back: "I think there will be great happiness, for if ever I saw a man who combined delicate tenderness to understand the heart of a woman, with quiet depth and manliness enough to satisfy her, it is Mr. Hawthorne." [51] After their marriage in June, 1842, the Hawthornes frequently welcomed Margaret to the "Old Manse" in Concord, and she seldom paid a visit to the Emersons without looking in upon their neighbors, the Hawthornes. In *The Dial,* she reviewed favorably Hawthorne's *Twice-Told Tales* and *Stories for Children,* and she predicted that he would continue to grow in power and favor with the public.

Why, one may then ask, did Hawthorne, after Margaret's death, paint, in his fictional portrait of Zenobia in *The Blithedale Romance,* a character so resembling Margaret in her least attractive guise that succeeding generations have come to regard the two as one and the same? Or why, one may ask with even greater puzzlement, did Hawthorne choose to malign her character and that of the young Italian nobleman whom she married? Granting even that Hawthorne himself never intended to publish his notebook remarks about Margaret's coarseness and her husband's lack of gentility, one still wonders how he could ever have harbored in the first place thoughts so in variance with those he expressed during Margaret's lifetime. Certainly, Katherine Anthony's explanation that he received the same kind of emotional satisfaction from vilifying Margaret that his Salem ancestor had derived from punishing witches lacks the force of argument.[52]

While it is true that Margaret tried to induce the Hawthornes to take Ellery and Ellen Channing under their roof when the carefree poet, who had married her younger sister, showed little inclination to provide a home on his own initiative; and while it is equally true that she interceded with Hawthorne to accept Charles Newcomb as a boarder, the record shows that Hawthorne understood her disinterested motives completely and thought even better of her for it. "Whether or not you bear a negative more easily than other people," Hawthorne wrote, "I certainly find it easier to give you one; because you do not peep at matters through a narrow chink, but can take my view as perfectly as your own." [53]

Perhaps it is foolish to blame a creative artist like Hawthorne for touching so closely upon actual life to accomplish the illusion of reality itself. If Zenobia possesses some of the idiosyncrasies that one must assuredly identify as Margaret's, her portrait also exhibited traces of Fanny Kemble and perhaps derived its physical attributes from the beautiful Almira Barlow, Margaret's friend and the attractive widow whose charms were by no means lost on the men at Brook Farm. Hawthorne's method of writing, as revealed in his notebooks, depended upon composites of both character and incident; and when he had breathed life into his compositions, they seemed to his readers individuals and events from the book of life instead of from the pages of fancy. So with the portrait of Zenobia—if one knows Margaret Fuller well enough, he will admire Hawthorne's handiwork as art; but as a picture of the flesh-and-blood woman, he will say along with Prufrock: "That is not it at all."

Though Margaret frequently came to Brook Farm to be gentle, dull, and silent, as she put it, she never changed her mind about becoming a member. The only association for her was still one of destinies. "It is a constellation, not a phalanxe, to which I belong," she once remarked.[54] Whenever she came to give one of her Conversations, she was warmly welcomed. One of the younger members, Georgiana Bruce, insisted on giving up her room to Margaret and brought her a breakfast tray in the morning. The married women stole time from her rest by coming to confide in her; one day as many as five appeared: their confessions "would make a cento, on one subject, in five parts," she later wrote in her journal.[55] Amusingly enough, she found herself in a new position at the Farm—that of a conservative—a condition she attributed to there being such a large proportion of young people. Her conservatism showed up during her Conversation in the annoyance she felt at first because of "the *sans-culotte* tendency" in manners, which led some of her listeners to throw themselves down on the floor while she spoke, and others to yawn or walk in and out at their pleasure. Thinking it over later, she decided it might be a challenge to hold forth under such conditions.

In the final analysis Margaret Fuller found so much to admire in the experiment of Ripley and his cohorts that only her sincere conviction of the necessity of an organic growth of society prevented her from accepting what appeared to be, for the time being at least, an exception to the rule that social organization always tends to force and thus injure human growth. She prized solitude and often needed its powers to restore her to health, but she could not consider herself a society of one as did Henry Thoreau, or insulate herself from human contact like Waldo Emerson. For her, individual was king, and she must guard herself jealously against submersion in the mass—there was simply no other way to achieve the kind of progress in which she believed.

V *Women and the West*

The early 1840's were crucial years in Margaret Fuller's development. Busy as she was with her editorial labors and her Conversations in Boston and at Brook Farm, she still felt restive and unfulfilled. Young Ellery Channing came closest perhaps to putting his finger on her problem. The young poet, whose perceptiveness in human relations so seldom is revealed in his verses, told her frankly that she was too idealistic. "Ideal people anticipate their lives," he said; "and they make themselves and everybody around them restless, by always being beforehand with themselves." [56] Margaret listened and agreed that he spoke truth, but was he not simply applying to her obscure life what is true "of every prophetic, of every tragic character"? Nevertheless she felt the weight of destiny heavy upon her; Goethe and some of her early experiences encouraged her to believe in fate and to attempt to probe into its mysteries. Talismans fascinated her: she chose the carbuncle for her stone and wore it whenever she wrote to certain friends; her seal-ring was impressed with the legend of Mercury; and her emblem was the sistrum, an instrument whose operation she likened to the play of her personality.

From Goethe, too, she borrowed the idea that every person "has a daemon, who is busy to confuse and limit his life." This daemon, which works instinctively in one's character, could neither be reached nor analyzed. One simply recognized that he had it. Margaret did, and she told Emerson, "With me, for weeks and months, the daemon works his will." [57] During these periods she seldom found it worth-while to undertake any serious project, preferring instead to read and study, the only record of her industry appearing in her letters or in the entries faithfully written down in her journal. At these moments she was most likely to reveal the stresses beneath her outward composure. Thus she wrote Charles Newcomb that she could not accept an invitation to visit him in her present state of mind and added, "I long to depart from a scene where most men seem only, ape-like, to grimace their parts, to some verdant solitude of 'truthful earnestness.'" [58]

When the "rye-bread" days, "all dull and damp without," came upon her, she thought of the friends who accepted her foibles without complaint and who remained loyal and steadfast through all her moods. She thought especially of Emerson, who had appeared at first to be "forever on stilts" with her but who had tested by now both his own and her ideas of friendship so thoroughly in conversation and corrrespondence that they could occasionally meet on the plane of familiarity. They were still, of course, far from complete agreement on the subject of friendship. "You go upon the idea that we must love most the most beauteous," she told him, "but this is not so. We love most that which by working most powerfully on our peculiar nature awakens most deeply and constantly in us the idea of beauty." [59]

One of these powerful incitements of which she spoke was the friendship between Bettina von Arnim and the young German poetess Karoline von Günderode. As early as 1838, when the romantic young Bettina's fictionalized account of Goethe's *Correspondence with a Child,* the purported record of her experiences with the poet, had appeared, Margaret had secured a copy. Her enthusiasm for the book spread until there was a cult among her women friends, and even Emerson succumbed to Bettina's charms. For the January, 1842, number of *The Dial,* Margaret wrote a lengthy article on Bettina and Günderode, and the same year she published anonymously in Boston a translation of part of the correspondence between the two young women under the title of *Günderode.* She had intended a much larger work, but the project was not finished until her friend Minna Wesselhoeft completed it in 1861.

Part of the charm Margaret found in the story of the two German women lay in the parallel between Günderode's influence upon her younger friend and Margaret's influence upon Sarah Clarke, Caroline Sturgis, Anna Barker, and others. Another reason for her fascination is that the two women served as admirable illustrations of Margaret's theories about the ideal, about nature and grace—in short, in the letters from abroad, she could find applications to her own life wherever she looked. She told William Channing: "Günderode is the ideal, Bettina nature. . . . There is a medium somewhere. Philip Sidney found it; others had it found for them by fate." [60] She had no way of telling what the future held for her; she only knew how difficult she found the middle course. "I am in danger of giving myself up to experiences," she writes at one point. At another, she says, "I am 'too fiery'. . . . Yet I think I am learning how to use life more wisely." [61]

Her friends seem to have agreed on one point at least. Both Emerson and William Channing called her a mystic. In Cincinnati James Clarke read her article in *The Dial* and wrote back: "I think you are disposed to mysticism, to Germanity. . . . I want to see Margaret Fuller herself—not Gunderode—not others." [62] She herself admitted: "I grow more and more what they call a mystic. Nothing interests me except listening for the secret harmonies of nature. I cannot bear plan, art, yet I see how godlike they are." [63]

She was interested—and accepted quickly—when James Clarke invited her to accompany him and his sister Sarah on a trip to the West. Clarke gave her fifty dollars to help expenses; and the journey, which began late in May, 1843, lasted into mid-September. They traveled first to Niagara Falls and then took the steamboat to Chicago. There William Clarke, another brother, joined them and served as a guide on an expedition through northern Illinois. Traveling by wagon, Margaret and her friends rumbled along country roads that seemed at times to disappear into nothingness. The prairie lands were almost entirely denuded of trees, although here and there crops covered the rolling terrain. They visited an Englishman in his prairie home on one occasion and a Unitarian minister on another. Both were pioneers in the frontier experience, yet appeared undaunted by the hardships of their new careers.

The Fourth of July was celebrated in the little town of Oregon, where her Uncle William lived. The visitors heard the usual patriotic oration—Margaret thought it "smacked loudly of Boston"—and participated in the day's festivities, which lacked perhaps some of the extravagance of preparations back home but certainly none of the fervor. Margaret was impressed by the opportunities for self-reliance and expansion that the West offered, but she was appalled by "the unfitness of the women for their new lot." Neither education nor experience, she could see, had done anything to prepare Eastern ladies for work or pleasure on the frontier. Everywhere, too, she found "the fatal spirit of imitation, of reference to European standards, [that] penetrates, and threatens to blight whatever of original growth might adorn the soil." [64] She wished she could have used these new experiences for her essay "The Great Lawsuit," which had just made its appearance as the lead article in the July *Dial.* Certainly there were fine illustrations here on every side to document the thesis that women become coarsened and man-like when they are deprived of the chance to find out their true nature as women.

Back again in Chicago, Margaret reread *Philip Van Artevelde* and was led by thoughts of the Flemish leader to envisage the future of her own land. When would America have a hero like Philip, she asked herself. She needs a new man:

> no thin Idealist, no coarse Realist, but a man whose eye reads the heavens while his feet step firmly on the ground. . . a man to whom this world is no mere spectacle, or fleeting shadow, but a great solemn game to be played with good heed. . . . A man who hives from the past, yet knows that its honey can but moderately avail him—when there is such a man for America, the thought which urges her on will be expressed.[65]

From Chicago Margaret journeyed with her party into Wisconsin, "still nearer the acorn that we were"; and finding Milwaukee and the surrounding area "almost as tame as New England," she pushed on alone to the Island of Mackinaw, where the Chippewa and Ottawa tribes had gathered to receive their annual payments from the United States government. Although the spectacle of lost dignity and fallen greatness saddened her, she had little confidence that "the stern Presbyterian, with his dogmas and his taskwork, the city circle and the college, with their niggard concessions and unfeeling stare" [66] would accomplish the work of redemption. She visited the Indians in their encampment, talked to the women in sign language, and compared what she experienced with her own eyes and what she had read in Schoolcraft and other authors who had written about the Indians from a more distant viewpoint. When it came time to depart, she made a mental comparison of civilization and the more instinctive existence she had just witnessed, and she decided that "the civilized man is a larger mind but a more imperfect nature than the savage." In the conflict between the two, there was no hope for the Indian unless the missionaries should become more liberal, the sharks of trade more human, and conscience be introduced into the flinty bosom of policy.

After Mackinaw, Margaret returned to her friends and Chicago; she was reluctant to leave the West but bowed to the inevitable with good grace. On the boat homeward, signs of Eastern culture began to appear: a shabby phrenologist reading bumps; a bereaved lover seeking religious consolation in Butler's *Analogy;* conversations about the doctrines of Fourier—homely indications all. But, in the afterglow of her recent experiences of watching sundown on the prairie and riding rapids in an Indian canoe, they seemed to be a bit tarnished.

Before going on to Boston, Margaret stopped at William Emerson's on Staten Island and visited with Henry Thoreau, who was staying as a tutor with the Emerson family. Henry listened attentively to descriptions of her summer adventures and encouraged her plans to turn journal notes into a book. Home once again, Margaret began to do research in the Harvard Library. Paying no attention to the stares of undergraduates and faculty, who found the presence of a woman in their sacred precincts a strange sight indeed, she kept steadily at her work throughout the winter. On May 23, her birthday, she was finally done. Although she had had no other purpose in mind than to share with others the footnotes of travel, she had unknowingly provided the means to enable her to enter into that larger sphere of action of which she had been dreaming.

Horace Greeley, the editor of the New York *Daily-Tribune,* had read Margaret's articles in *The Dial,* and his wife had sung Margaret's praises after attending some of her Conversations. Enthusiastic about all things Western, Greeley liked Margaret's book, *Summer on the Lakes,* when it was published; and he offered her a job as literary critic on his paper to fill the place of Albert Brisbane, who had resigned to devote his full time to socialism and enterprises like Brook Farm. Measured by "the ample fields of the West," New England had seemed "a poor shady little nook" to Margaret; but now that she was home and enjoying the splendor of autumn, she told Henry James, Sr., that it seemed "as good a place as any in the world." It wrenched her heart, therefore, to leave it; but since her family were now able to get along without her close supervision, she told her brothers that she would accept Mr. Greeley's offer. They agreed to assume the burden she had been carrying, and she laid plans to move to New York.

Before making the change, Margaret had one task to finish. During October and November, while spending seven delightful weeks of rest with Caroline Sturgis near the Hudson at Fishkill, New York, she revised her *Dial* article, "The Great Lawsuit," expanding it with added illustrations and arguments until it reached book length, and retitling it *Woman in the Nineteenth Century*. Upon completing it in mid-November, she wrote Emerson, "I . . . have spun out my thread as long and many-colored as was pleasing." [67] The same day her letter to William H. Channing expressed a feeling of "delightful glow, as if I had put a good deal of my true life in it; as if, suppose I went away now, the measure of my footprint would be left on the earth." [68] To Orestes Brownson, writing with all the fervor of his newly found Catholicism in the October issue of his *Boston Quarterly Review* about her *Summer on the Lakes*, she had indeed left footprints: "No person has appeared among us whose conversation and morals have done more to corrupt the minds and hearts of our Boston community. For religion she substitutes art; for the Divinity . . . she would give us merely the Beautiful." Only the year before, Emerson had paid her fairer tribute: "We are taught by her how lifeless and outward we were, what poor Laplanders burrowing under the snows of prudence and pedantry." [69]

CHAPTER 4

Champion of Truth and Human Good

> ". . . my foot is on the earth and I wish to
> walk over it until my wings be grown. I
> will use my microscope as well as my
> telescope."—M.F.

WHEN MARGARET FULLER left her native Cambridge,
putting down "the golden lyre" to pick up "the slow pen"
as a journalist in New York City, she entered a world that most
New Englanders looked upon with disfavor. New Yorkers were
too worldly for most transcendentalists, but gentlemen like
Oliver Wendell Holmes found them boorish. By the same token,
New Yorkers looked upon New Englanders, especially Bostonians, without enthusiasm. Gothamites could see no value whatever in the fogs and mists of transcendental vagaries, and Edgar
Allan Poe in particular showed his disdain for Brahmin preten-
sions by labeling the residents of Boston "Frogpondians."

Adding further to the dismay of Margaret's friends over her
removal to New York was her choice of vocation. Women had
been associated with journalism in one or another capacity
before her, but no woman had ever invaded the world of the
fourth estate as a member of the working press. Her New
England friends were shocked by her daring. Emerson did not
attempt to dissuade her, but neither did he lend encouragement.[1]
Margaret brushed all objections aside because she was determined to eradicate sectional differences if she could and to
continue the work of interpreting European culture to Americans
that she had begun while she was editor of *The Dial*. She never
had cause to regret her decision. In her "Farewell" to New York,
just before her departure for England, she left a record of what
the city had meant to her. "New York is the focus," she wrote,

"the point where American and European interests converge. There is no topic of general interest to men, that will not betimes be brought before the thinker by the quick turning of the wheel." In New York, she added, ". . . twenty months have presented me with a richer and more varied exercise for thought and life, than twenty years could in any other part of these United States." [2]

She spoke without exaggeration. Living and working in New York between December 1, 1844, and August 1, 1846, she grew intellectually and emotionally, shedding much of the mystical "Germanity" that had so distressed her friends in New England. She acquired knowledge and skills and developed her analytic and critical powers. She met people from various fields and spheres of influence and learned to separate sincerity from sham and hypocrisy; she also saw at first hand the failings of democracy and looked behind the façade of institutional forgetfulness at the victims of human weakness and venality. Like a schoolgirl, she gave her heart away and then recoiled from the open display of passion that her ardor evoked; when her beloved withdrew from this counterfeit of love, she bore her chalice of woe in hurt resignation. Finally, she took her place among the "Literati" of the City, having earned, both at home and abroad, a reputation as a challenging personality and as defender of the cause of woman's rights. In all respects, it was indeed a rich and varied experience.

I *The* Tribune

When Margaret Fuller joined the staff of the New York *Tribune*, it was in its fourth year of existence under the one-man rule of Horace Greeley, whose entire life was wrapped up in its liberal Whig policies. A Vermont farm boy with all the country man's love for the city, Greeley virtually carried the *Tribune* about in the capacious topper that drew attention to him wherever he went. Honest and outspoken to the degree that he had recently been horsewhipped by an irate political foe, he had just paid court damages to James Fenimore Cooper for a libelous review of one of Cooper's *Leatherstocking Tales.*

Greeley had dedicated himself wholeheartedly to the moral improvement of the reading public. A vegetarian and a Grahamite, who occasionally backslid at public banquets, he loved causes: the fate of the working man; the North American Phalanx at Red Bank, New Jersey; and even the rights of women. Hiring a woman to serve as literary editor of a daily newspaper was without precedent; but it seemed feasible to him because he wished to woo female readers who were finding it very difficult to secure worth-while reading materials in the daily papers published by Greeley's competitors. The *Sun*, the *Transcript*, and the *Herald* specialized in lurid ads and sensational reports; Greeley's plan was to concentrate on news about literature, the arts and social questions.

Margaret Fuller was hired to write three articles a week for the daily edition of the *Tribune*, two on literary subjects and one on social matters. Many of these were subsequently reprinted in the weekly and semi-weekly editions. She was also responsible for reviewing the foreign press and culling from it items that she considered useful for her employer's editorial columns. Greeley gave her complete freedom of action. She could discuss new books or American editions of foreign works, write reviews of music and drama, editorialize on philanthropic activities, or report the latest developments in science. She felt most at home where literature and art were concerned, but she lost no time in gaining experience at first hand about the charitable institutions, hospitals, and prisons of the city. In the company of William H. Channing or Lydia Child, both of them dedicated reformers, she visited Sing Sing, Blackwell's Island and prison, and Bellevue Hospital. She sat by the bedside of patients or visited with prisoners in their cells to hear their stories and learn what she might do to help them.

So far as science was concerned, she lacked training to make any real contributions; but she never flinched from reviewing scientific books and gave consistent support to the necessity of employing a scientific attitude toward investigations of phenomena. Her logical reasoning and intellectual acuteness as well as her regard for truth protected her, on the one side, from prejudice when knowledge was lacking; and, on the other, from leaping to conclusions before all available evidence had been examined. She deplored the resistance of religious orthodoxy to scientific research, but she also displayed some inconsistency in her failure to submit clairvoyance and magnetism to the scrutiny of science.[3]

Since Horace Greeley's wife had invited Margaret to live at their spacious country home at Turtle Bay on the East River, he had plenty of opportunity to become acquainted with her methods of work. They did not always meet with his approval because Margaret was not accustomed to his giddy pace. When the "black jailer" or the "vulture with iron talons"—her epithets for migraine—seized her, or when her spine ached excruciatingly, Margaret could not work, a source of some frustration to Greeley, who swallowed up daily deadlines and could not understand Margaret's taking as long to write one column as he took to write ten. He fretted a bit about her preparing copy at home because he loved every minute that he spent at Nassau Street and found it difficult to understand why Margaret did not have the same affection for *Tribune* headquarters that he had.

As a matter of fact, Margaret found her situation, both at work and at home, entirely satisfactory. Several months after moving in with the Greeleys, she wrote her brother Eugene in New Orleans that she had never been so well situated. She lived in "Castle Rackrent" style, she told Eugene, but she was comfortable and enjoyed the affection of both her employer and his wife. "Mr. Greeley I like, nay more, love," she wrote. "He is, in his habits, a—plebeian; in his heart, a noble man. His abilities, in his own way, are great. He believes in mine to a surprising extent. We are true friends." [4] In another letter, she confessed to her friend Mary Rotch, "He teaches me things, which my own influence on those, who have hitherto approached me, has prevented me from learning." [5]

Greeley, on his part, soon came to admire Margaret. In time he learned that her weaknesses and faults were small in comparison with the greatness of her mind and soul. Where truth and human good were concerned, he found her "a most fearless and unselfish champion." He called her "the most remarkable, and in some respects the greatest, woman whom America has yet known" and applauded her courage and outspokenness, although he thought her theories about women's rights must remain abstractions as long as she demanded to be treated like any other member of the "weaker" sex. Teasing her unmercifully whenever she sought special privilege as a woman, he liked to repeat her off-quoted statement about women: "Let them be Sea-Captains, if you will!"

There is no doubt whatever that he thought highly of her *Woman in the Nineteenth Century*, which he and his partner, McElrath, published in February, 1845. "Margaret's book is going to *sell*," he told Rufus Griswold. "I tell you it has the real stuff in it."[6] Many years later, he took the time to be more specific about Margaret's bold challenge to the world of respectability: "If not the clearest and most logical, it was the loftiest and most commanding assertion yet made of the right of Woman to be regarded as an independent, intelligent rational being, entitled to an equal voice in framing and modifying the laws she is required to obey, and in controlling and disposing of the property she has inherited or aided to acquire."[7]

Even before her book appeared, Margaret's articles in the *Tribune* had drawn favorable notice from readers. What might be expected from her in the way of objectivity and honesty became evident from her first piece of criticism—a review of the second series of *Essays* of her good friend Emerson. Although her respect for truth and for Emerson himself influenced her to praise his purity of mind and integrity of purpose, she felt compelled to voice some dissatisfaction that Emerson had not fulfilled his genius. "We doubt," she wrote, "this friend raised himself too early to the perpendicular and did not lie along the ground long enough to hear the secret whispers of our parent life. We could wish he might be thrown by conflicts on the lap of mother earth, to see if he would not rise again with added powers."[8]

In this very first effort, Margaret revealed the critical plan that underlies all of the literary articles that she wrote for the *Tribune*. Later on she gave it written expression in her article "English Writers Little Known Here."[9] In essence her method consisted of dividing literature into three classes: the work of genius; the work of gentlemen or scholars, who serve as audience to genius and as interpreters to the multitude; and finally the work of energetic men who have something valuable to tell their contemporaries. She believed in bringing to the notice of the reading public writers of these last two classes but did not consider it important to criticize them formally. She did measure, however, the writers of the first class. After attempting first of all to determine the law of each writer's genius, she then judged him by it and finally compared him with a recognized standard of past genius like Dante, Shakespeare, or Goethe.[10]

Although she called herself a member of "the gentle Affirmative School" of criticism, having learned from German critics like Schlegel and Tieck to appreciate the "good qualities" of an artist, she also saw the importance of "the uses of severe criticism, and of just censure, especially in a time and place so degraded by venal and indiscriminate praise as the present." [11] She rejected the "system of mutual adulation and organized puff" that characterized contemporary criticism; she was determined to "tell the whole truth, as well as nothing but the truth" with the one stipulation that all "sternness be in the spirit of love." [12]

She was always seeking means by which to reconcile the ideal with the real. Admonishing her readers to remember that "positive existence is only effigy of the ideal and that nothing is honourable which does not advance the reign of beauty," [13] she attempted to break down the barriers that Puritan morality and otherworldliness had erected between Americans and the world of senses. Her romantic propensity toward the ideal gradually fused with an organic theory of art "woven and assimilated from the earth and sky" of the artist's own being and environment.[14] These two, when joined to a broad historical view of art that envisioned American and British literature as an integral part of *Weltliteratur*, provided the rationale for a truly creditable list of critical judgments on American, British, and European literature.[15]

Finding New Yorkers badly in need of a re-education concerning the French, she wrote an account of DeVigny, Eugene Sue, Balzac, and George Sand under the heading "French Novelists of the Day." All four had been known to her for some time, and she was able to keep *au courant* through the French newspapers and periodicals that came to her desk in the *Tribune* office. None of these artists fell into her first class of writers who possessed genius: DeVigny was a dilettante, Sue spoke only to his contemporaries, Balzac repelled with his materialism, Sand had not yet written any memorable books. True to her critical purpose, the article was more descriptive and informative than analytic.[16]

When she turned her attention to "Modern British Poets," she concentrated on the leading writers of the Romantic movement. Campbell, Moore, and Scott were treated as "singers"; Crabbe, Shelley, and Byron as "poets of suffering"; Southey, Wordsworth, and Coleridge as "the pilot-minds of the age." Although she made the common mistake of her time in overrating Southey, she showed critical insight in relegating Leigh Hunt to the men of talent. Shelley's *Prometheus* was not to her taste, but she cherished the "Hymn to Intellectual Beauty" and claimed closer kinship to him than to "the nearest companions of life actual." For some reason not disclosed in any of her papers, she neglected any mention of John Keats, although she knew of his brother George through James Clarke and tutored the poet's niece in her own home. Where Byron was concerned, she was able to separate the poseur from the artist and looked to the future to assign Byron high place among poets. Wordsworth lacked the versatility of the greatest artists, but he possessed "the delicacy of perception, the universality of feeling which distinguish Shakespeare and the three or four other poets of the first class." Coleridge, she very perceptively noted, can "suggest to an infinite degree. . . . To the unprepared he is nothing, to the prepared, everything." [17]

British prose writers did not escape her critical eye, and she took issue with Carlyle's efforts to dragoon his readers into accepting his views while lauding Landor for treating his readers gently in an incomparably fine prose style. But it was in her reviews of American authors and their works that she showed her true mettle. Although she was almost an exact contemporary of the authors whom she criticized and therefore lacked the valuable perspective that distance usually gives, she demonstrated remarkably keen insight in her evaluations of writers like Brown, Cooper, Bryant, Longfellow, Lowell, and Poe. When she fell short of her own high critical standards, it was usually where she wished to introduce new writers like Ellery Channing or Cornelius Mathews. Even then, she was too honest to claim artistic merit for sentiments that she believed the reading public might appreciate.

She was fully aware that the genius of a new country like the United States differed from that of a settled nation like Great Britain. Her organic theory of art demanded, moreover, that an American literature be compounded of the spirit of freedom and the open frontiers of her native land. "Fresh currents of life" and "an original idea" must reinvigorate the nation, she prophesied, before it could speak with authentic voice. That day would come only when the American people "prize moral and intellectual no less highly than political freedom." [18]

She saw some of these symptoms of national rebirth in the growing efforts to bring about social reform, in the investigations of American history by contemporary scholars like Prescott and Bancroft, and in the spiritual teachings of divines and philosophers like Dr. Channing and Emerson. But she knew only too well from her editorial experience with *The Dial* and from her Western travels that "the sluggard intellect" of the continent had not yet been fully aroused to see the loveliness of America's natural beauties or to test the pulse of national life and feel the surging power and restless energy of its people. She acknowledged the charm and geniality of Irving and credited Fitz-Greene Halleck and Nathaniel Willis with the elegance and wit of society poets, but she reserved her more serious comments for Longfellow, Lowell, and Poe.

When she first reviewed Longfellow's work in 1845, she confessed to feeling cool toward him because of "the exaggerated praises that have been bestowed upon him." Although she felt no inclination to press the charge of plagiarism, which seemed obvious to her, she penetrated to the heart of Longfellow's weakness in the comment, "Nature with him, whether human or external, is always seen through the windows of literature." [19] Longfellow never bothered to comment on her remarks, although she reiterated the charges of imitativeness and artificiality in her article on "American Literature," which appeared the following year.

James Russell Lowell possessed a less charitable nature. When Margaret commented, in the same article, that Lowell was "absolutely wanting in the true spirit and tone of poesy" and that "his verse is stereotyped; his thought sounds no depth; and posterity will not remember him," [20] Lowell was stung so badly that he resolved to pay her back. In his "A Fable for Critics," he had the last word by caricaturing Margaret as Miranda, "the whole of whose being's a capital I." Since Lowell had published only two volumes of early poems when Margaret wrote her criticism and since he retained fewer than half of them when he collected his works, her judgment appears more than likely to have offended him because of its honesty and truthfulness than for any other reason. [21]

Her criticism of Poe, though by no means lacking in penetration, was hardly definitive. With the exception of his "Raven," she found something lacking in his poems: "they are all fragments—*fyttes* upon the lyre, almost all of which leave us something to desire or demand." She praised his powers of invention in the tale, but she showed either ignorance of Poe's theories or blindness toward his shortcomings by suggesting in two reviews that he undertake a long "metaphysical romance." Her statement, "He needs a sustained flight and a fair range to show what his powers really are," [22] makes little sense when viewed against "The Philosophy of Composition" or Poe's failure with *The Narrative of Arthur Gordon Pym*. She was on firmer ground when she called Hawthorne "the best writer of the day" and chided her countrymen for their failure to remember Charles Brockden Brown. Melville seems to have been known to her only through *Typee*, which she reviewed moderately, giving Melville credit for having written from experience his "pretty and spirited pictures" and commending his "quick and arch manner." [23]

Among contemporary critics Margaret Fuller alone possessed the breadth of knowledge necessary to deal with literature ranging from the classics to the latest publications of authors in Britain, on the Continent, or on the American scene. No one could match her theoretical grounding in European standards of literary criticism, and few—Poe was a notable exception—showed the kind of interest that she manifested in current American literature. After she made the acquaintance of Evert A. Duyckinck, an editor with the firm of Wiley and Putnam, she joined forces with the youthful leader of the "Young America" movement and did what she could in her capacity as a *Tribune* editor to assist him in fostering American letters. A wealthy man with a huge library and a large circle of literary friends, Duyckinck was responsible for the Library of Choice Reading and the Library of American Books published by Wiley and Putnam. Through his urging Margaret collected her critical pieces, and Duyckinck brought them out in two volumes in 1846 under the title of *Papers on Literature and Art*.[24] Her essay "American Literature," the only new piece in the miscellanies, was actually part of Duyckinck's program to bring about an improved native literature.

Although most of Margaret's articles for the *Tribune* dealt with literature, art, music, or the drama, she did not neglect the social problems of which she had spoken so frankly in her book *Woman in the Nineteenth Century*. After its appearance in February, 1845, she became a marked figure, pointed out in public as the author of "*that* book on women" and criticized in private because of the candor of her views and because she had dared to touch on such matters as prostitution and marital infidelity. But Margaret was not upset by public disapproval; she was concerned rather with the ignorant and depraved women who languished in New York's prisons and houses of correction. She spent Christmas Eve with the women prisoners at Sing Sing and shared other holidays with them as well. After she had surveyed the city's remedial and corrective institutions, she published her findings in the *Tribune*. What is more, she tried to raise money to establish a house of refuge for young women and gave unstintingly of her time to numerous other efforts to reform New York's inefficient rehabilitation services.

As her contacts among the social outcasts and poverty-stricken of the community widened, a new note of realism began to enter her reporting. Her comments lost none of their accuracy or pertinence but gained in force and compression. She increased her research concerning the causes of want and discrimination and studied seriously the problems of New York's huge immigrant population. Her articles "Capital Punishment," "What Fits a Man to Be a Voter?" "The Irish Character," and "Prison Discipline" reveal not only the diversity of her new knowledge and experience but also the steady growth of her social conscience. *Woman in the Nineteenth Century* was a protest against a double social and moral standard, but it had been based largely on the vicarious experience Margaret had gained from her reading; now she had actual experience to support her conclusions and to lend further strength to her conviction that women must fight to secure their rightful inheritance in society. More than ever, she was a revolutionary waiting for a great cause; the time when she would see her wish granted was not far distant.

II *James Nathan*

Margaret's New York experiences were not limited to philanthropy and her duties on the *Tribune*. Shortly after coming to live with the Greeleys, she met at a party an attractive man of her own age whose friendship helped to fill the many lonely hours of her first months as a stranger in New York. The man's name was James Nathan. Born of a Jewish family in Holstein, Nathan had come to America as a penniless immigrant in 1830. When Margaret first met him, he was well established in the commission business in New York, although, by temperament, he preferred music and literature to the daily round of buying and selling.

Throughout the spring of 1845 Margaret and the gentle, blue-eyed dreamer, who wrote verses and played *lieder* upon his guitar for her, spent as much time together as their busy schedules would permit. They wrote letters back and forth, composing them early in the morning or late at night, before and after their working day. The inevitable happened: they fell in love.[25] Although Margaret had felt she was in love before—James Clarke, George Davis, Sam Ward, and Charles Newcomb had all stirred her feelings—none of them had ever aroused the emotion she felt for James Nathan. For the first time in her life she was deeply and passionately in love, although she was still unable to play a lover's role except as she had dreamed or read about it.

She soon put her entire trust in Nathan. And he was wise enough to court her as a woman, though, by his own account, he was first attracted by her "high intellectuality, purity of sentiment and winning conversation." At first he used to call upon Margaret at Turtle Bay, where they could stroll about the grounds of the Greeley estate or sit and read poetry to each other. But after the Greeleys showed their disapproval, he and Margaret arranged to meet at the home of friends like Lydia Child, at the studio of Christopher Cranch, or at the office of her physician, Dr. Leger. On other occasions they attended the opera or went to concerts and the art museums together, finding in music and painting an expression of the romantic sentiments that bound them together.

Spring came early that year. Their love for each other seemed matter fit for an idyll until one day Margaret wrote a more than usually impassioned letter to Nathan with results she did not anticipate. "I wish, I long to be human but divinely human," she said. "Are you my guardian to domesticate me in the body, and attach it more firmly to the earth?"[26] Misconstruing her sentiment and giving literal significance to her figures of speech, Nathan responded with a passion that awakened Margaret rudely from love's fair dream. Fearful and saddened, she reproached him in her next letter for showing his "lower" self. He apologized immediately and gave her his puppy, Josey, as a peace offering to make up for his breach of etiquette. But his ardor had cooled. They continued to write, but the course of love, judged by the alternating tone of complaint and reconciliation in Margaret's letters, ran over rapids from this time forward.

Finally, in the middle of April, Margaret received a confidential letter from Nathan explaining that he had to go abroad. At first she was startled and concluded that Nathan had ceased to care for her, but then "pride and self-love" were swept aside, and she thought only of his hopes and wished that they might be realized. April passed into May and Nathan delayed his departure in response to her importuning. Margaret confided the news of his going away to Mrs. Greeley, who took a less wide-eyed view of Nathan's action; and when Margaret told Nathan what she had done, he became very upset. But still she kept faith, although she sensed a growing coolness in his letters. "Perhaps I am, as you say, too sensitive," she wrote him, "and, in that case it is well we are to separate now, for we are already too near to be easy or well, if the unison be broken." [27] But when June and the moment of Nathan's leave-taking arrived, she had to summon all her courage not to give way to her feelings. She sent Nathan on his way with a parting gift of Shelley's poems and went home to put into a letter what she could not say at the time of parting.

Throughout June and the summer months that followed, she kept busy with her writing when she was not attending meetings with various welfare groups or visiting the public institutions of the city—anything to keep her mind occupied. She welcomed her mother for a visit and then, shortly afterward, Emerson. After they had gone, she found in the Greeley's new baby, Pickie, someone to cherish and take her mind off herself. All this time, her letters followed Nathan on his travels. At first he responded, asking Margaret in one letter to secure a letter of introduction for him from George Bancroft, who was now Secretary of the Navy, in another, to arrange with Horace Greeley to publish his travel notes. Margaret took care of his requests promptly and informed him that she had accomplished what he had asked. But Nathan wrote only once more between September and the end of the year. Margaret's letter to him on Christmas Eve admitted to feeling somewhat jealous because she was finally beginning to realize that he had left her to seek "new impressions"—something that she had never felt the need of as long as he had been with her.

Before the first of the year arrived, she moved into town because she had become increasingly lonely. She met Cassius Clay, the publisher of *The True American*, whose press in Kentucky had been destroyed by a mob who opposed his antislavery ideas. Clay's sentiments and personality so impressed Margaret that she wrote a piece about him for the *Tribune*. The Danish adventurer Harro Harring made an equally deep impression upon her. She listened to his talk about Garibaldi and revolution in Europe and gave him money to print his novel *Dolores*, when his publishers became fearful of his opinions and reneged on their contract. Later she wrote a strong piece entitled "Publishers and Authors" for her column in the *Tribune* which urged writers and publishers to get together so that the sanctity of contracts might be protected.

Men like Clay and Harring were stimulating, but they could not make up for the pain that throbbed constantly in Margaret's bosom. By now, she was fairly certain that Nathan never intended to return to her. When she wrote him near the end of April, she had not heard from him for four months, and he wrote only briefly after that. Back with the Greeleys in the early spring, she could not stand the sight of surroundings made dear by memories of love so she took rooms by herself in Brooklyn Heights. There she wrote Nathan in July about her plans to leave New York and to travel abroad. She made it plain that she expected either to see him personally or to find a letter from him when she arrived in London; but the tone of the letter is businesslike and suggests that she was not too sanguine about ever seeing him again.

III *"The Literati"*

Early in the winter following James Nathan's departure for Europe, Margaret had moved from the Greeley's into town, first to a boarding house and then to more pleasant quarters on Amity Place, where she could invite friends and entertain. "I make many acquaintance and see many amusing people and some who are very friendly to me," she wrote Nathan.[28] Although she concealed her loneliness from those around her, she could not put the same heart into her new ties as she had into those of former years. Still, she did not agree with Lydia Child, who told her that it was too much trouble and a waste of time to go out at all. "I think she lives at disadvantage by keeping so entirely apart from the common stream of things," Margaret wrote another friend.[29] Thus she found it increasingly pleasant, though she never stayed late because of work the next day, to attend the literary gatherings and parties to which her growing reputation as an author and conversationalist had won her entrée.

From her rooms on Amity Place it was only a short walk to Waverly Place and the home of Anne Lynch, an acquaintance of Margaret's days in Providence and now one of New York City's most enthusiastic hostesses to budding genius. At Miss Lynch's *soirées* there was always a mixed group of authors, wits, artists, critics, and dilettantes, some parrying thrusts at their latest work or delivering critical ripostes of their own. Edgar Allan Poe often attended these affairs, and his description in *The Lady's Book* of "The Literati of New York City" reads like a roll call of those persons, including Anne Lynch herself, who were most frequently in attendance. "New York literature may be taken as a fair representation of that of the country at large," he wrote. "The city itself is a focus of American letters. Its artists include, perhaps, one fourth of all in America, and the influence they exert on their brethren, if seemingly silent, is none the less extensive and decisive." [30]

One of the not-so-silent visitors to be found where the "Literati" gathered was Margaret's friend Evert Duyckinck, who was always on the lookout for native writers of promise. Another was the author of *Hope Leslie* and *The Linwoods,* Catherine Sedgwick, a member of a distinguished Massachusetts family who spent much of her time in New York, where she could observe metropolitan society and take part in its reform movements. Still another was Elizabeth Oakes Smith, wife of the Down East Yankee, Seba Smith, and in her own right a novelist and sometime poet. Anna Cora Mowatt, who defied convention by writing, staging, and producing her own play *Fashion,* a satirical comedy directed against the manners of Gotham society, joined the "Literati" on occasion. A much more faithful attendant was the beautiful Frances Sargent Osgood, whose airy fancies and dancing eyes so fascinated Poe that he made a fool of himself and in his article in *Godey's Lady's Book* gave her far more space than writers of greater talent received. Women were definitely in the majority, but the appearance of Nathaniel Willis or Charles Fenno Hoffman or of artists like Christopher Cranch prevented these affairs from becoming exclusively circles for discussion of women's rights or for gossip about fashions and reputations. Even Horace Greeley dropped in occasionally to take part in the conversation, and then matters were very likely to veer around to a discussion of social questions.

Edgar Allan Poe was undoubtedly the most striking personality among the men who attended these meetings of New York's "Literati." Margaret noted that when he stood up, his slender figure robed in decent but shabby black, and read in his low, melodious voice from the long slips of blue paper on which he had written his poems, there was always rapt attention. She and Poe conversed at different times but never really became friendly. Poe was a ladies' man; but he found Margaret's habit of looking at him "one moment earnestly in the face, at the next seeming to look only within her own spirit, or at the wall" rather disconcerting.[31] She, on the other hand, never really exerted herself to win Poe's attention.

When Poe's *Tales* had been published the previous June, she had reviewed them briefly but favorably for the *Tribune;* and later, when *The Raven and Other Poems* appeared in November, she had written a more extensive and generally commendatory criticism. Poe was pleased by both pieces and reciprocated by treating her work with fairness and good taste in his series of articles on "The Literati," which began to appear in May and ran through November, 1846. In this "critical gossip," as he dubbed his series, Poe occasionally showed his dislike for what he described as "the Emerson and Hudson coterie—the Longfellow clique, one and all—the cabal of the 'N. American Review.'"[32] For example, young Ellery Channing, who had come to New York to work on the *Tribune,* drew Poe's fire as a member of the "Bobby Button" school. Channing, Poe added, had been inoculated with "virus from Tennyson" and outdid Carlyle in "quaintness and obscurity." With the exception of a brief reference to Margaret's poetry as being "tainted with the affectation of the transcendentalists," Poe treated her work as an author and critic quite generously.

Margaret's review of Longfellow, which Poe characterized as "one of the very few reviews of Longfellow's poems, ever published in America, of which the critics have not had abundant reason to be ashamed," naturally endeared her to Poe as a critic. But he was also surprisingly tolerant of her book on women, since his views on social reform and feminism differed radically from hers. "*Woman in the Nineteenth Century* is a book which few women in the country could have written, and no woman in the country would have published, with the exception of Miss Fuller," wrote Poe.[33] He agreed with only part of Margaret's conclusions because he thought she neglected certain intentions of the Deity regarding sexual differences. "She judges woman by the heart and intellect of Miss Fuller," he added, "but there are not more than one or two dozen Miss Fullers on the whole face of the earth." [34]

Declaring that Margaret possessed "high genius," Poe described her essay as "nervous, forcible, thoughtful, suggestive, brilliant," although he felt duty-bound to cite a few instances "from among a multitude of wilful murders committed by Miss Fuller on the American of President Polk." Despite these defects and "her frequent unjustifiable Carlyleisms," Poe found Margaret's style "one of the very best with which I am acquainted. In general effect, I know no style which surpasses it. It is singularly piquant, vivid, terse, bold, luminous; leaving details out of sight, it is everything that a style need be." [35]

Shortly after these comments were published, two events occurred to make Poe furious and to cause him to alter his opinions of Margaret Fuller. One related to a personal relationship by which Margaret became involved in Poe's private life; the other had to do with Poe's hurt pride as an author.

It is difficult to explain why Margaret allowed herself to accompany Anne Lynch to Poe's cottage at Fordham to retrieve some letters that Fanny Osgood had unwisely written to Poe. [36] Mrs. Osgood was no particular friend; Margaret must simply have thought it her duty to stand up for one of her sex, or perhaps she still remembered her own feeling of angry helplessness when James Nathan had refused to return her letters. In any case, the unpleasant task was accomplished, without incident, but Margaret had made an enemy.

Not long after, Margaret gave Poe another incentive to downgrade his opinion of her. When her *Papers on Literature and Art* appeared in the summer of 1846, it contained her essay on "American Literature"; but the essay itself carried no mention at all of Poe. Some of Poe's remarks in the "Literati" article had evidently nettled Margaret, for the haste with which she had to put her materials together certainly does not explain adequately such a serious omission, especially since she was already on record as admiring Poe and was able to find space in her essay for minor poet and dramatist Cornelius Mathews.

Poe was no more inclined to accept a slight like this than was James Russell Lowell. In January of the same year that Lowell's *Fable for Critics* appeared, Poe wrote to George W. Eveleth:

"I agree with you only in part as regards Miss Fuller. She has some general but no critical powers. . . . She is grossly dishonest. She abuses Lowell, for example, (the best of our poets, perhaps) on account of a personal quarrel with him. She has omitted all mention of me for the same reason—although, a short time before the issue of her book, she praised me highly in the Tribune. . . . In a word, she is an ill-tempered and very inconsistent old maid— avoid her." [37] Later in October, Poe asked Sarah Whitman, his beloved "Helen" and another of Margaret's friends from the Providence days, why she associated with Margaret and others among the "Literati" who were not his friends.[38] Finally, in February, 1849, after having written an anonymous review of Lowell's *Fable* for the *Southern Literary Messenger*, Poe suggested to his friend Frederick Thomas that Margaret, "that detestable old maid," was responsible for Lowell's "writing satire against mankind in general, with Margaret Fuller and her protégé, Cornelius Mathews, in particular." [39]

Posterity has agreed that Lowell's *Fable* deserves to live; it has permitted Poe's "Literati" to fade into the limbo of scholarly curiosities. While Lowell refused to be content with portraits of the merely talented writers of the New England scene and painted better word pictures than perhaps even he knew of the truly significant writers of his day, Poe recorded temporary opinions of a group who, for the most part, lacked the skill and genius to make lasting contributions to the world of literature. In the final analysis, neither critic took particular pains to probe into the secret of Margaret Fuller's genius. Certainly Poe showed little awareness of her remarkable probity. Although it is perhaps technically true that she deserved to be considered among his "Literati," in a much larger sense she really did not have much in common with the ladies who composed verse for the literary annuals or who contributed sentimental articles to the women's magazines. Hers was a more exalted mission—to free the minds of men and women from the bonds of convention and to teach them justice. Careful perusal of what she wrote during the year and a half that she served as an editor of the New York *Daily-Tribune* proves how earnestly she sought to accomplish that purpose.

CHAPTER 5

European Dream and Journey's End

"I have wished to be natural and true,
but the world was not in harmony with
me—nothing came right for me."—M.F.

AS EARLY AS SEPTEMBER, 1845, Marcus and Rebecca
Spring, the wealthy, philanthropic couple who befriended
Margaret Fuller during her stay in New York, evidently spoke
to her about accompanying them to Europe. She was strongly
attracted to the idea, and her letters to James Nathan during the
following winter refer to the possibility of such a trip. After
receiving assurance from Horace Greeley that she might write
for the *Tribune* while she was abroad, she finally decided to take
the momentous step. She had saved a thousand dollars and
needed five hundred more if she were to travel with any feeling
of security; she decided to ask for help from her old friend Sam
Ward, who had given up the life of an artist and was now a
partner in his father's banking firm.

In her letter Margaret reminded Sam that it was just ten years
since she had been compelled to abandon her trip to Europe
with him and the Farrars. How much, she wondered, had she
lost by not going. "It would have given my genius wings," she
thought.[1] Now, she commented somewhat sadly, her character
was pretty well formed. The best she could hope for was to add
to her store of knowledge; and a career—if one were still possible
for her—lay somewhere in journalism rather than among the creative arts. Still, all knowledge was worth-while, and she would
appreciate his extending her credit until she could repay him
from her salary as a *Tribune* correspondent. Sam obliged, and
the last obstacle to her plans was removed.

She returned to Cambridge late in July to bid goodbye to her family and friends. On her last day at home, Emerson drove from Concord to pay his respects and to give her a letter of introduction to Thomas Carlyle.[2] Emerson was especially pleased that Margaret was finally to realize her dream of foreign travel, and the two parted without the slightest intimation that they were seeing each other for the last time. On August 1, 1846, Margaret sailed with her friends aboard the *Cambria* for England; the final chapter of her life was about to begin and end in strange lands, for she was never again to set foot on her native soil.

I *England and Scotland*

After a record crossing of ten days and sixteen hours, the *Cambria* reached Liverpool on August 12. Margaret began immediately to fill a notebook with descriptions and details of the people and places which she thought would be of interest to readers in New York. These entries were later expanded and developed in the letters that she wrote for publication in the *Tribune;* and her brother later collected many of them in the volume *At Home and Abroad* which, together with the copious extracts in the *Memoirs* edited by Emerson and her friends Clarke and Channing, provides today's reader with a fairly complete record of her experiences during the nearly three months that she spent in England and Scotland.

From the very beginning she discovered in England "a greater range of interesting character among the men" than in America, although, as she wrote Caroline Sturgis, "I do not find, indeed, any so valuable as three or four among the most marked we have known."[3] Amused by "the mechanical" talk about character that she heard in English homes, she wrote in her notes: "With all the abuses of America, we have one advantage which outweighs them all. Most persons reject the privilege, but it is, really, possible for one to grow."[4] She was appalled at the poverty and squalor which Melville was to depict so realistically in *Redburn,* but she saw some hope for improvement among the lower social classes in the Mechanics' Institutes that were being established to take care of girls as well as boys. She was heartened also to hear an address on self-improvement in which quotations from *The Dial* were cited. As a matter of fact, she was quite pleasantly surprised to find that English readers thought very highly of the journal which her New York acquaintances so often had regarded as merely amusing.

The industrial face of England as it displayed itself in Liverpool, Manchester, and Birmingham depressed Margaret and her friends. Chester was more to their liking with its rich historical associations, and the lake country was all that Margaret had anticipated, although Wordsworth's home at Rydal Mount seemed less romantic than her imagination had pictured it. At Ambleside, Margaret visited Harriet Martineau for more than a week. There was still a coolness in Miss Martineau's manner because she had not forgotten Margaret's taking her to task some years previously, but the two women found one subject on which they could agree: mesmerism. Harriet had just recently been restored to health almost miraculously by the treatment of England's prince of mesmerists, Mr. Atkinson, whom Margaret had met in London; and Margaret could testify to the good services of her New York physician, Dr. Leger, who had helped her to walk straight by "dunamizing" her, Leger's term to distinguish his own particular method of therapy from that of other specialists in magnetism.[5]

Another resident of the Ambleside area stood high in Margaret's affections. At seventy-six Wordsworth bore a benign and reverend appearance, but Margaret was pleased to find that his seclusion among the quiet northern hills had not completely shut him off from concern for the struggling unfortunates of the cities, for he spoke more liberally about the Corn Laws than she had expected. In Edinburgh, she chatted with DeQuincey, whose views, though out of touch with the present, were expressed with eloquence and urbanity. DeQuincey's grace contrasted with the vigorous and fiery manner of Dr. Thomas Chalmers, now in the last year of his life, but still a determined and forward-looking pioneer of the Free Church. She was equally impressed by the liberality of mind and breadth of knowledge of Dr. Andrew Combe, who gained her full sympathy for the shabby treatment he had been accorded by American publishers.

At Rowarden on Loch Lomond in Scotland, Margaret and the Springs rested at the little inn in preparation for the four-mile ascent of Ben Lomond. Becoming separated during the climb from her only companion, Marcus Spring, Margaret became lost on the mountain and was forced to spend the night alone and unprotected against the cold and dampness until a searching party of shepherds sent out by Mr. Spring discovered her in the early dawn. A near-tragic experience, it provided a kind of catharsis; for Margaret had received in Edinburgh, just before departing for the Highlands, a letter written by James Nathan informing her of his engagement to a German girl. In her diary she had written with restrained bitterness the following remarks:

> I understand more and more the character of the *tribes*. I shall write a sketch of it and turn the whole to account in a literary way, since the affections and ideal hopes are so unproductive. I care not. I am resolved to take such disappointments more lightly than I have. I ought not to regret having thought other of "humans" than they deserve.[6]

But Nathan's betrayal still rankled. Alone in the blackness of the mountain top, her mind filled with doubts and questions, with possible death hiding in the gloom about her, she finally emerged from the dark night of the soul with the memory of love burned from her mind. She sent word afterward to Mr. Delf, Nathan's agent in London, and asked him to tell Nathan that she had received his letter but "was too much involved in the routine of visiting and receiving visitors to allow her mind a moment's repose to reply to it."[7] So much for the rites of pride; the episode was finished, and love would find a cooler welcome in the future.

Leaving the Highlands, Margaret's party returned to Edinburgh by way of Glasgow, which seemed like an inferno to her; the stamp of misery on the faces of the citizenry, especially the women, filled her with grief that was only partially assuaged by the knowledge that Scotland's manufacturing cities, "burning focuses of grief and vice," also sheltered "centres of intellectual life." From Edinburgh the travelers journeyed south, passing through York and Sheffield and visiting scenes of royalty—Warwick Castle and Shakespeare's birthplace in Stratford, which Margaret was surprised to find had been a shrine "only for forty years," the belated recognition of the Bard being due, she reasoned properly, to the prior appreciation of the Germans.

In Birmingham she heard speeches by George Dawson, a leader among the popular party whom she preferred to James Martineau, Harriet's brother, who was an intellectual but nevertheless, Margaret thought, a "partially developed man." Neither could compare in sympathy and persuasive power with W. J.

Fox, the English reformer. The three men reminded her of reformers like William H. Channing and Theodore Parker. None could match Channing in "pure eloquence and communication of spiritual beauty," nor were any Parker's equal in "fulness and sustained flow"; but all three, she thought, surpassed her American friends in their capacity to relate theory to practical concerns.

The end of September had arrived before the travelers finally reached London. Parliament was in session; and for an observer like Margaret, who could not stomach "the shocking inhumanity of exclusiveness," the spectacle of royalty parading through streets thronged by beggars and out-of-work ruffians was not one she cared to see.[8] Actually she had little time to visit "the inexhaustible studio" of treasures which lay before her. The response to her letters of introduction was so warm, she wrote Emerson, "that I had hardly time to dress, and none to sleep, during all the weeks I was in London." The English edition of her *Papers on Literature and Art* was reviewed in glowing terms by *The Critic*, which singled out her "quickness of apprehension" and "sound judgment" for particular attention.[9] The reading public had already discovered her *Woman in the Nineteenth Century,* and she received several invitations to contribute to English periodicals. But she had neither time nor inclination to write for them because she was kept busy either by sightseeing or by social engagements in London.

A visit to Hampstead to see the aged Joanna Baillie was first on her list. She marveled at the octogenarian's Roman strength and praised her "singleness of mind." Mary and William Howitt, the publishers of the *People's Journal,* became her intimate friends; and one of the contributors to their magazine, Joseph Mazzini, so impressed her with his patriotism and unselfish love for his native Italy, from which he had been driven to become the leader of England's colony of Italian refugees, that she was sealed to his cause almost from the moment she met him.

True to the promise that Emerson had exacted from him, Carlyle called upon Margaret and invited her to his home at 5 Cheyne Row. The first time she went, Carlyle put on his best behavior, telling witty stories and drawing character sketches that made Margaret laugh without restraint. "Carlyle is worth a thousand of you for that," she wrote Emerson; "he is not ashamed to laugh, when he is amused, but goes on in a cordial human fashion."[10] She had her next opportunity to see the Carlyles at a dinner party. One of the guests was the author George Lewes, who would one day win the heart of Mary Ann Evans, better known to posterity as George Eliot. Margaret disliked Lewes, whom she described as "a witty, French, flippant sort of man"; but she was pleased whenever he managed to take the conversation away from Carlyle, who was in one of his "more acrid moods" and who dominated the evening with judgments that both wearied and caused her to disagree with him. Adding to her frustration was the information that Lewes, whom she considered shallow and irreligious, was writing a life of Goethe, the task which she had been forced to set aside.

Before leaving England, the Springs invited the Carlyles and Joseph Mazzini to their apartments. Margaret was succeeding in drawing out Mazzini, who had begun to speak earnestly of his plan for freeing Italy from her rulers, until Carlyle began to harangue them. At first Mazzini tried to protest in his gentle, courteous way, but Carlyle was in a mood to hold forth so that the others were forced into silence while he discussed heroism and other pet doctrines. Even though his arrogance was hard to suffer, Margaret could not help liking Carlyle, for she knew that it was not self-love or overweening pride but a kind of titanic energy and exuberance that drove him to ride down opposition to his ideas. Carlyle liked her too. "Margaret is an excellent soul," he wrote Emerson. "Since she went, I have been reading some of her Papers in a new Book we have got: greatly superior to all I knew before; in fact the undeniable utterances . . . of a true heroic mind;—altogether unique, so far as I know, among the Writing Women of this generation; rare enough too, God knows, among the writing Men." [11]

Time grew short, and there were people whom Margaret had still to meet. But Tennyson was out of town and the Brownings were newlyweds honeymooning in Italy. So Margaret took some precious hours to visit the galleries and museums. There was no opportunity to view any private collections, except one of Turner's, but she did manage to get to the Dulwich and the National galleries and to Hampton Court. For the British Museum she had only one day. The net result of this peeping-Tom act was that she felt all the more tantalized by glimpses of "the riches of existence," and she began to sense for the first time how much of color and tone she had missed by being cut off from the world streams of great art. Her remarks on the

Allston exhibition and her gushing comments over black-and-white reproductions came back to make her blush, but she resolved to re-educate herself by taking advantage of the treasures soon to come.

II *France and Italy*

By November Margaret was situated in Paris. She wrote her mother, "I have been obliged to give a great deal of time to French, in order to gain the power of speaking, without which I might as usefully be in a well as here." [12] Although she made rapid progress, she begrudged the precious hours stolen from the pitifully few days that had been set aside for "doing" Paris. She made a schedule and adhered to it ruthlessly, but she felt unsatisfied. "My steps have not been fortunate in Paris, as they were in England," she wrote Emerson. "I need, to initiate me into various little secrets of the place and time . . . some friend, such as I do not find here." [13] She attended academy lectures and court balls, visited the picture galleries and the Chamber of Deputies; but at night she fell into bed, sleepless and hungering for experiences that she had been unable to squeeze into her busy day.

When she attended the French theater, she thought it much more alive than the English. She saw the gifted tragedienne Rachel perform on several occasions and came away each time marveling at the intensity of her performance. Rose Cheny amused her as Clarissa Harlowe, and the dialogue of the plays that she saw in the little theaters convinced her that the French stage possessed "a sparkle of wit" unknown to the rest of the world. Although the orchestration at the different opera houses satisfied her, she was critical of the vocal parts. She visited the *Opera Comique* only once, and even the Italian opera failed to arouse her admiration. "I find the tolerable intolerable in music," she reported to her readers in the *Tribune*.

Again, as in London, she discovered that her reputation had gone before her. *La Revue Indépendante* had already published her essay on American literature and was planning to print *Woman in the Nineteenth Century*. The editor asked her to consider a position as correspondent when she returned to America, and Margaret promised to give serious thought to the proposition. She went to call on Lamennais, to whom she had a letter of introduction, and was overjoyed to find with him "a somewhat citizen-looking" man, who turned out to be the poet Béranger. "There are men who need no flourish of trumpets to announce their coming," she wrote in her dispatch to the *Tribune*. "They are the true kings . . . the mind of the age is the historian of their passage." [14] Lamennais's former disciple, George Sand, finally returned from her country home late in January; and Margaret, who wanted to see her more than any other person in Paris, called upon her at the Place d'Orléans. "I never liked a woman better," she wrote Elizabeth Hoar.

The hectic disarray of a household that included George ·Sand's daughter, Solange, who was about to be married, gentlemen of her mother's circle, and the sickly Chopin, did not dismay Margaret. There was something admirable, she thought, in everything George Sand did. "She needs no defence," she wrote, "but only to be understood, for she has bravely acted out her nature, and always with good intentions." [15] Later, she visited Chopin, who had succeeded Franz Liszt in George Sand's affections. Chopin talked with her and played several of his compositions, and she thought she understood what Adam Mickiewicz had meant by saying, "Chopin talks with spirit, and gives us the Ariel view of the universe." [16]

Polish poet Mickiewicz became one of Margaret's dearest friends in Europe. A revolutionary in exile since his student days, who had already established himself as one of Europe's leading writers through his historical poems and his epic, *Pan Tadeusz*, Mickiewicz had begun actively in the 1840's to work for the political and social reconstruction of all Europe. Stirred and inspired by the theories of transcendentalism—chiefly as he found them expressed in Emerson's essays—Mickiewicz had for several years, from his post as professor of Slavic literatures at the Collège de France in Paris, been preaching the same ideas of self-expression and equality of opportunity for women as well as men to which Margaret was dedicated.

Unfortunately, Margaret did not meet Mickiewicz until the middle of February when her stay in Paris was nearly finished. She wrote Emerson, "I found in him the man I had long wished to see, with the intellect and passions in due proportion for a full and healthy being, with a soul constantly inspiring. . . . How much time had I wasted on others which I might have given to this real and important relation." [17] Throughout the remaining months of 1847, she and Mickiewicz kept in touch with each other by letter; and after he arrived in Rome in February, 1848, they saw each other frequently while the struggle for Roman independence dragged on to its fateful conclusion. The correspondence which records the sincere affection that these two friends felt for each other also reveals that Margaret intended to share actively in the plans that Mickiewicz was making to help with the work of liberating the oppressed people of Italy.[18] The letters to the New York *Tribune* which she wrote during the latter half of 1847 and the early months of 1848 also carry a new emphasis on human rights that very likely came from Mickiewicz as much as from Mazzini or from the actual events taking place before her eyes

Although her experiences in England and later those in Rome and in Florence enabled her to see that Paris was the "focus of the intellectual activity of Europe," [19] Margaret was not blinded to the sufferings of the poor or to the unrest of a populace dangerously near the point of starvation. Much as she thought Fourier was in error because he made "the soul the result of health of body, instead of body the clothing of soul," she rejoiced to see that some progress was being made, in the name of his doctrines, to alleviate by practical means the terrible social evils that she saw everywhere in Paris. Revolution, she conjectured, might not be far off. "While Louis Philippe lives," she wrote, "the gases may not burst up to flame, but the need of radical measures of reform is strongly felt in France; and the time will come, before long, when such will be imperatively demanded." [20]

On February 25, 1847, Margaret left Paris for Italy. Traveling by way of Lyons and Avignon, where she waded through snow to visit the tomb of Petrarch's celebrated Laura, her party passed through Arles on the way to Marseilles, where they boarded a steamer to Genoa and then suffered through a miserably cold trip of thirty hours. From Genoa they went to Leghorn and Pisa and from there by steamer to Naples, which they reached after a near-fatal collision with the mail boat, an incident that served only to increase Margaret's lifetime dread of the sea. Naples was cold at first, a carbon copy of a New England spring with a villainous east wind, but here Margaret could finally say, "I have at last found my Italy." Despite its dirt and degradation, Naples appeared to her to be a true symbol of "the divine aspect

of nature" that God had seen fit to lavish on the Italian
countryside.

April found Margaret in Rome, living on the Corso and watching torch-bearing processions wending their way through to the
Quirinal to thank Pius IX for his efforts on behalf of representative government in Rome. She viewed the pomps of Holy Week
"and found them less imposing than an habitual acquaintance
with the church itself." At night she could hear the owls hooting
in the Colosseum. She wrote William H. Channing that she had
undergone a change in her point of view. "Art is not important
to me now," she said. "I like only what little I find that is tran-
scendently good, and even with that feel very familiar and calm.
I take interest in the state of the people, their manners, the state
of the race in them." [21] But in order to keep abreast of the work
of her contemporaries, she visited the studios faithfully so that
she could report to her countrymen what American artists were
doing abroad. Through her letters to the *Tribune*, as well as
through personal letters to friends at home, she played an important role in helping to prepare a favorable climate for painters
like Luther Terry, Thomas Hicks, and her old friend Christopher
Cranch and for the sculptor Thomas Crawford, who won praise
from her for his action in joining the Roman Guard. [22] In June
when she reached Florence, she visited Horatio Greenough and
Hiram Powers at their studios, and she thought both men were
doing work of which their country could be proud.

In Florence Margaret became acquainted with the Marchioness Arconati Visconti, who befriended her then and later when
Margaret hardly knew where to turn or whom to call upon for
help and advice. After a month's visit, she and the Springs left
Florence, visiting Bologna on their way to Venice, where the
sight of the nobility entertaining at a birthday party brought to
her mind thoughts of "the Stuarts, Bourbons, Bonapartes, here in
Italy" and caused her to pray "that other names, when the pos-
sessors have power without the heart to use it for the emancipa-
tion of mankind, might be added to the list, and other princes,
more rich in blood than brain, might come to enjoy a perpetual
villeggiatura in Italy." [23] The contagion of revolution was influ-
encing her thinking.

When she fell ill in Venice because of all her traveling and
sightseeing, Margaret convinced the Springs to go on without

her. Then she settled back to recover her strength and enjoy the city. Before the end of July, she was well again and on her way, stopping at Vicenza, Verona, Mantua, Lago di Garda, and Brescia and learning "more than ever in any previous ten days of my existence." After catching a fever in Brescia, she resolutely pushed on to Milan and arrived there drawn and weak but on the way to recovery. The high point of her visit was a meeting with Manzoni, whose *I Promessi Sposi* (1825-26) she had admired for many years. White-haired now, Manzoni impressed her with "the habitual elevation of his thoughts"; but she was also aware that the gentle old man symbolized Italy's romantic past—a past far removed from the unrest and clangor of contemporary times. Other voices in Milan spoke to her of disturbances in Rome and of the formation of a National Guard. Austrian troops were reported to be moving against Ferrara. There was an air of expectancy and she found it "impossible not to hope" that the results would benefit the cause of freedom.

From Milan Margaret traveled during August to Switzerland. On her return she spent a fortnight at Lake Como with her friend the Marchioness Visconti, who introduced her to the Polish-born Princess Radzivill, one of Europe's glamorous women and one intimate with circles of experience that were charming and entirely new to Margaret. Leaving the lovely lake region was hard, but Margaret returned to Milan and from there proceeded to Florence, where she rested from her fatiguing journey at the home of Joseph Mozier, an American businessman turned sculptor. Although she wrote home, "I would not give a pin to live in Florence," she found the art treasures of the city beautiful beyond her fondest dreams and she enjoyed a pleasant circle of friends. She spoke French fluently now, though incorrectly, and she was beginning to show increasing facility in Italian. "Italy receives me as a long-lost child," she wrote Elizabeth Hoar; and she grew critical of those of her countrymen in Italy who never bothered to learn anything about Italian life or literature while they had the opportunity.

All about her in Tuscany, hopes ran high that the Austrian rule might at last be overthrown because the people were encouraged by recent actions of the Pope and the Grand Duke. Margaret urged her American readers to give some expression of sympathy. "This cause is OURS, above all others," she wrote; "we ought to show that we feel it to be so. . . . The soul of our nation need not wait for its government; these things are better done by individuals." [24] Now she wished she had had more sympathy for the abolitionists when she had had the opportunity, and she remembered that she had done little more than speak piously of working for the annexation of Texas.[25] She had always spoken up concerning matters of conviction about public affairs; now she was convinced that one also had to take action.

III   *Ossoli and Revolution*

Margaret returned to Rome about the middle of October and settled down by herself to a quiet existence in a small apartment on the Corso. Her plans called for another four of five months in Rome to collect materials for a book about Italy before returning to America to write and publish her discoveries. She was pinched for money and driven to many economies in order to stretch the four hundred dollars that remained of her savings. Though she could not foresee what lay ahead, she was optimistic and hoped to begin to enjoy herself. But her peace and quiet proved to be short-lived; romance and revolution, side by side, came looking for her; and when they found her, they brought momentous changes into her life.

The previous spring while visiting St. Peter's during Holy Week services, Margaret had met by chance a young Italian nobleman. Their casual acquaintance had ripened enough during the months prior to Margaret's departure for Venice for the Marchese Giovanni Angelo Ossoli to propose marriage to her. But although she claimed, at a later date, that she loved him, Margaret had politely refused her Italian suitor, who was nearly ten years younger than she and lacking in both the intellectual and educational attainments that she had come almost to take for granted in her friends. Besides, she had only recently been able to look back philosophically at her experience with James Nathan. She was not anxious to fall in love again; and her own words, written when she had been preparing the manuscript for her book on women, came back to her as a warning: "How terrible must be the tragedy of a woman who awakes to find that she has given herself wholly to a person for whom she is not eternally fitted! I cannot look on marriage as on the other experiments of life: it is the one grand type that should be kept forever sacred." [26]

But Ossoli resumed his suit when Margaret returned to Rome in the fall of 1847, and soon they were constantly in each other's company. The young nobleman, though lacking both money and training, came from a good family whose political sentiments were of course conservative. But under Margaret's tutelage Ossoli soon became an apostle for Roman liberty. With a foot in both camps, he was able to keep Margaret—and later Mazzini when that patriot came to Rome to direct personally its struggle for freedom—informed of developments in the conservative party. When volunteers were needed later on, Ossoli joined the Roman Civic Guard and comported himself courageously when siege was laid to the Eternal City. His manliness and utter simplicity, coupled with his unselfish devotion, finally overcame any scruples Margaret had, and sometime during that autumn she took him as a lover. "Woman is born for love, and it is impossible to turn her from seeking it," she had once written. Wisely or not, she had now fulfilled her own prophecy.

Life goes well, she wrote happily several weeks before Christmas. During the hazy autumnal days she explored points of interest about Rome; on Monday evenings she entertained her closest friends in Rome, the Cranchs and the William Storys; the other evenings were spent writing and studying, with Ossoli sitting quietly by, watching her with adoring eyes. "I have not been so well," she told her mother, "since I was a child, nor so happy ever, as during the last six weeks." [27] Her friends, including Henry Hedge, who was visiting in Rome that winter, all remarked at the change brought about by her new-found happiness.

But suddenly the tone of her letters changed. She wrote Emerson, "I am tired of keeping myself up in the water without corks, and without strength to swim. I should like to go to sleep, and be born again into a state where my young life should not be prematurely taxed." [28] She had discovered that she was going to have a baby, and all at once the full significance of her situation had come home to her. Without a husband, nearly penniless and facing the very real possibility of not being able to continue her work, she looked into a grim future. Love had consequences for her, she now discovered, as well as for others who had tried to play its game without paying the price. Although she could not reveal her secret to anyone, she wrote Caroline Sturgis, now about to be securely married, "I am a poor magnet, with power to be wounded by the bodies I attract . . . with this year, I enter upon a sphere of my destiny so difficult, that I, at present, see no way out, except through the gates of death." [29]

To add to her depression, the rainy season began in mid-December. For nearly three months torrential rains poured almost daily on the city so that Margaret's little apartment, dark even when the sun was shining, now seemed more like a cave or prison cell. Her health broke down under the double burden of carrying a child and mental unrest, and she remained close to her fire, a virtual prisoner until Carnival time. The only note of cheer during late January and February was the reported success of the revolutionary movement. In Rome, Leghorn, and Genoa, the people were revolting; in Milan during a popular uprising, the Austrians killed eighty citizens, whose deaths ignited revolutionary fervor everywhere.

By the end of March, Margaret's black hour seems to have lightened. Although her fortunes were still "dark and tangled," she threw herself on God's bounty and trusted to His keeping. It seems likely that she and Ossoli decided to marry at this time. Although her friend Emelyn Story, who provides the only written account describing the details of Margaret's romance,[30] seems to think that the marriage took place in December, 1847, shortly after the death of Ossoli's father, Margaret's correspondence during this time leads to the conclusion that the marriage was delayed until early April.[31] It was secret of course, and it most likely took place in one of the neighboring towns so that the records might not easily come to light; for, if it were known that Ossoli had married a woman who was both a Protestant and a liberal, his chances of remaining in Rome or of inheriting a share of his father's estate would be lost.

Spring of 1848 brought good news to Margaret and other supporters of the revolution. Prince Metternick had been forced to resign in Austria; Louis Philippe had abdicated in France and had barely escaped to England; Naples had revolted. While she looked on in the company of Mickiewicz, who occupied rooms in the same building on the Corso where she lived, Austrian arms were dragged through the streets of Rome and then burned. The double-headed Austrian eagle was torn down, and in its place an Italian one, inscribed with the words ALTA ITALIA, was raised. There was dancing in the streets, and young men rushed to volunteer for military service. Mazzini, Margaret heard, had returned to Milan from his seventeen years of exile and had been warmly welcomed by Milanese patriots. Everywhere "the real men were rising to power."

On April 1, it seemed that Italy was free, but Margaret's letter to the *Tribune* cautioned against accepting as true what seemed to be "too speedy a realization of hope." Still her heart was cheered, and she felt reinvigorated by nature's awakening. "Gods themselves walk on earth, here in the Italian spring," [32] she wrote; but she was saddened by what she considered a lack of "moral courage" in Pius IX, the Roman pontiff, who had earlier impressed her with his leadership and support of the popular cause. On April 29, at a consistory of the College of Cardinals, Pio Nono disassociated himself from the war movement. Dismayed at the headlong surge of the people to obtain freedom by any means at their disposal, the Pope, who had envisioned a peaceful and more gradual regeneration of Italy with the Papacy guiding and directing its progress, recoiled from the bloodshed that had occurred and withdrew his earlier leadership and encouragement.

Although she had shared the sentiments expressed in Mazzini's open letter to the Pope the previous December—a letter pleading with the Pontiff to become the center around which Young Italy could rally—Margaret now looked to other men and to stronger measures to make "the year 1850 a year of true jubilee to Italy." She rejected Emerson's proposal to return to America. How could he so easily "close the book of European society"? she asked him.[33] The spirit that had made America great was now asleep there, she wrote to the *Tribune*. In Europe, it had come alive again, and she wanted to play her part in seeing that it did not die. If she could not help in the actual work itself, she would gladly be its historian.[34]

By the end of May, Margaret was nearly six months pregnant. She had kept her secret well, but now she decided to have her baby in the country. After a month's stay in Aquila, she went in July to the little town of Rieti in the Abruzzi, that land of heart's desire for both priest and soldier in Ernest Hemingway's memoir of another love and war in Italy. While she waited for the baby, she continued work on the book about her European experiences. It would take at least three months to finish, she wrote her friend Madame Arconati. Her radicalism had not abated. "I am no bigoted Republican," she said, "yet I think that form of government will eventually pervade the civilized world. Italy may not be ripe for it yet, but I doubt if she finds peace earlier. . . ."[35]

To Emerson, she wrote happily about her situation among the peasants, "They are people whom I could love and live with. Bread and grapes among them would suffice me."[36] She was proud that she was going to bear Ossoli's child; but sometimes fear of approaching motherhood and worries about money—her letters to Horace Greeley and to her brother Richard for help had not yet been answered—cast shadows on her happiness. On one occasion at least her fears found voice. "I am too rough and blurred an image of the Creator, to become a bestower of life," she wrote humbly, but then found consolation in the philosophy that had always sustained her. "Yet, if I refuse to be anything else than my highest self, the true beauty will finally glow out in fullness."[37]

On September 5, 1848, Margaret and Giovanni had a son. At the last moment, Ossoli, who had expected to be called to Bologna with the Civic Guard, was able to be at Margaret's side; but he could stay only for a few days. When she was able to return to Rome in November, Margaret made arrangements to leave the baby with a nurse in Rieti because both she and Ossoli still felt the need to conceal their marriage.

Back in Rome, Margaret took lodgings in one room on the Piazza Barberini, the best accommodations that she and Ossoli could afford. She lived, for a time, on a hundred dollars borrowed from an American friend. After a silence of six months, she once again resumed reporting the revolution to the readers of the *Tribune*, but because of a mixup in mailing, she still had not received the advance she was expecting from Horace Greeley. Rome was largely deserted now. The tourists had all gone; and the populace, who depended on their trade, experienced great suffering, especially since Count Rossi, the prime minister, imposed increasingly stringent measures upon them. Shortly after her return, Rossi was assassinated; and when a crowd of citizens, struggling to see the Pope, were fired upon by some members of the Swiss Guard, they retaliated and killed the Pope's confessor. Pope Pius fled secretly to Gaeta after this had occurred, and Rome was left without a government until the Roman Republic was proclaimed in February, 1849.

A dedicated revolutionary by this time, Margaret found herself torn between thoughts of the revolution and consideration for her child. Her brother Richard wrote to her about joining him and his wife in the American West, and Margaret thought how ironic the proposal was. She wrote him back: "It is something if one can get free foot-hold on the earth, so as not to be jostled out of hearing the music, if there should be any spirits in the air to make such." [38] She received a visit from Mazzini, who was now a member of the Assembly and an elected citizen of Rome, and they talked about the difficulties piling up against the revolution. She wished to help him even if it meant giving her life. Later, she hurried to Rieti and spent a month with her baby. Christened Angelo Eugene Philip, the child was well and thriving, and she returned to Rome satisfied that he was receiving good care.

During April, May, and June, Margaret's life was so eventful that she had no time to think of the baby or of herself. After the Catholic powers of Europe decided to restore papal sovereignty in Rome, the president of the French Republic, Louis Napoleon, sent an expeditionary force to Italy under General Nicholas Oudinot, which landed and seized Civita Vecchia near Rome on April 25. Expecting little resistance from the Romans, Oudinot received a sturdy denial to his request to turn over the City. On April 30 he laid siege to it, and Garibaldi's troops dug in, prepared to resist to the death. That very day, the Princess Belgiojoso, an Italian noblewoman who had sacrificed everything for the Republican cause, named Margaret the regolatrice of the Hospital of the Fate Bene Fratelli. From then on, night and day, Margaret labored with the sick, attending men in the wards, comforting the dying, and talking with the less seriously wounded. According to Mrs. Emelyn Story, who sometimes accompanied her during her rounds, Margaret's gift for easing the men's suffering was remarkable. "How long will the Signora stay? When will the Signora come again?" they cried whenever she appeared.

The impression most people had of her at the time, according to Mrs. Story, was that "she was a mild saint and a ministering angel." [39] Love, motherhood, and a broad experience of human suffering had done much to temper Margaret's haughty spirit and to gentle her naturally impulsive and critical nature. She was certainly not ready for canonization, but her deeds now made Lowell's caviling and Poe's ill-tempered criticism seem puerile and uncharitable. [40] One of the truest indications of the manner in which the crucible of war was melting down her sharper edges and refining her spirit is to be found in the increased sensitivity to the needs of humanity and in the heightened power and compassion with which that sensitivity was expressed in the letters that she posted to the *Tribune* during the final days of the Roman Republic.

Sometime during the siege, when she thought perhaps Ossoli, who was stationed at a fortification in the wall under active bombardment, and she might die, Margaret told Emelyn Story about her secret marriage and the whereabouts of her son. She also entrusted certain confidential papers relating to her marriage to Mrs. Story's keeping.[41] Later these were returned unopened to Margaret and were presumably lost at sea when the shipwreck that took her life occurred.

Despite the bravery of Rome's defenders, the city could not withstand the heavy cannonading of French batteries. Late in June the walls were finally breached, and on July 4 the invaders entered the city shortly after Garibaldi had escaped with his remaining forces to fight elsewhere. Soon after, General Oudinot issued a proclamation ordering all foreigners who had helped the Republic to be out of Rome in twenty-four hours. Although it nearly broke her heart to leave the wounded men behind and to see the ravaged city on its knees, Margaret's letter of June 10 to the *Tribune* indicates that she and Ossoli intended to comply with the order. Through the assistance of Lewis Cass, the United States Envoy in Rome, she and her husband succeeded in getting transportation out of the city. Saddened by the news she had just received of the death of Pickie, Horace Greeley's son, she was in for another shock when she arrived at Rieti. She and Ossoli found Angelo nearly dead from malnutrition because his nurse, who had received neither money nor instructions from Margaret during the siege, had not fed him properly.

Fortunately Angelo recovered. When he was well enough to travel, they went for a rest to Perugia and later to Florence. There was now no reason to conceal their marriage. With the failure of the revolution, Ossoli's hopes of receiving a post in the Republican government or of becoming reconciled with his own family were destroyed. Return to America seemed the best solution to their problems, and Margaret wrote her mother and sister Ellen and her friends like Caroline Tappan, Sarah Clarke, William H. Channing, and Emerson about her marriage. She wrote proudly about her husband's love for her and their child, and she sounded his praises, although she never pretended that he was something he was not.

There is in some of her letters, however, concern for what her friends might think of Ossoli. She wrote her sister Ellen, "I expect that to many of my friends, Mr. Emerson for one, he will be nothing, and they will not understand that I should have life in common with him." [42] Emerson was quite noncommittal when he reported the news of Margaret's family to his brother William;[43] but there was some buzzing in Boston and New York circles, where some, no particular friends of Margaret, found it necessary to revise their image of her. Among her friends in Europe, her revelation occasioned some surprise because it was unexpected; but she received only expressions of warm understanding from people like the Storys, Madame Arconati, and Horatio Greenough, who arranged for the Ossolis to remain in Florence when the police showed signs of forcing them to leave. The Marchesa Arconati wrote an especially gracious letter to Margaret, whose reply somewhat self-consciously stated, ". . . it looks to me silly for a radical like me to be carrying a title. . . . It is a sort of thing that does not naturally belong to me and unsustained by fortune, is but a souvenir even for Ossoli." [44] When Christmas Day came—the first and last of the little family together—the "dragon of poverty" still breathed upon her and her loved ones; and her immediate hopes for the diffusion of freedom in Europe lay blasted. Her letter describing that day ends on a sombre note—"God bless all good and bad tonight and save me from despair."

IV Homeward Bound

The Italian spring was "as good as Paradise," even in Florence. "How dreadful it will be hereafter to shiver and pine up to the middle of May," Margaret wrote Lewis Cass. "Yet I must go brave that and many an ugly thing beside." [45] Surrounded by friends and the treasures of the past, during her last months in Italy Margaret could never free herself completely from doubts and premonitions about the future. In the mornings she worked away busily at her history in order to have a finished manuscript for a publisher when she arrived in America. She had already alerted Emerson to find a suitable one. Afternoons, she took long walks with Giovanni into the hills and valleys surrounding Florence. Evenings were for company.

The Brownings had now become good friends. Elizabeth Browning was with child, and the maternal bond drew Margaret to her quite naturally. Elizabeth soon came to love Margaret for her spiritual and thoughtful qualities but never thought much of her writing except for the occasional flash of wit in her letters. Margaret thought Robert Browning a "genuine Saxon." His full tide of talk exhilarated and warmed her and told her many things she wanted to know, but he did not exert himself to draw her out. On his part, it was enough for Browning that his wife loved Margaret. He loved her too and respected her dedication and courage.[46]

Late in April, Margaret began to complete her plans for departure. She borrowed three hundred dollars on a note, using Marcus Spring as security. Originally she planned to take the packet ship *Argo* from Le Havre when it returned from America, but it was wrecked at sea. She decided then to sail on a merchant ship. After inspecting the nearly new merchantman *Elizabeth* as it lay at berth in Leghorn, she booked passage for four, having decided that she would need a girl to help with Angelo during the two months' voyage. Horace Sumner, Charles Sumner's younger brother, who had been exchanging English lessons with Ossoli for instruction in Italian, also accompanied them. On May 17, Captain Hasty and his wife welcomed the passengers aboard, and they set sail under fair skies with their cargo of rags and Italian marble.

But misfortune soon struck. Captain Hasty died of smallpox on June 2 and was buried in the harbor of Gibraltar. Adverse winds caused the *Elizabeth* to lie over for a week, so that it was June 9 before they set sail again under the command of the first mate, Mr. Bangs. Two days later Angelo came down with smallpox but gradually recovered. Margaret finally found time to look at her manuscript, and Ossoli and Sumner resumed their language lessons while young Angelo played with the goat that had been brought along for fresh milk. Heaven seemed finally to be smiling on them, and Margaret began to lose some of the dread that her fear of the sea had aroused.

On July 18 the *Elizabeth* stood off the Jersey coast at noon, and the mate told his passengers he would have them safely ashore the next morning in New York. In the storm that suddenly blew up that evening, the ship went off course; at four in the morning it ran aground off Fire Island. The heavy marble in the hold broke through the ship's bottom, and the turbulent waves began to pound away at her. The shore was only several hundred yards away, but it might as well have been several miles as long as the gale continued to rage. Figures appeared on the beach, but no one made any attempt to get help to the stranded ship. Finally there was a lull about nine o'clock. Later Mrs. Hasty was propelled safely ashore on a plank by Mr. Davis, the second mate. About noon the order was given to abandon ship, but Margaret refused to be separated from her husband and child. All but four of the crew jumped overboard, leaving the Ossolis huddling by themselves on the tossing deck. At three the steward took Angelo and promised to save him or die. Then the ship broke up and all were thrown overboard. Angelo's dead body and that of the steward were washed ashore minutes later, but two of the sailors managed to save themselves. Margaret and Ossoli were never seen again.

The report of Margaret's death came as a shock to all who knew her. Henry Thoreau hurried to the scene of the wreck, but no trace of the bodies of Margaret or her husband could be found. Some of Margaret's letters and diaries were recovered, but her manuscript history had been swallowed by the sea. The long voyage was done; at the very last, irony continued to exercise its relentless rule. With security almost in reach, the "old ninny-woman, Fate," had stepped in to snatch away the most precious gift of all—life.

CHAPTER 6

The Fruits of Self-Culture

"All criticism should be poetic; unpredictable; superseding, as every new thought does, all foregone thoughts, and making a new light on the whole world."
—R. W. EMERSON

MARGARET FULLER believed at one time that her thoughts required at least an "enchanter's mirror" or a "magic ring" to embody them. But just as Whittier learned to tune his own reed without Milton's "gift divine" and Marvell's "wit and graceful song," so Margaret became humble enough to court excellence in others when she discovered that she herself possessed neither the sceptre nor the lyre of creative genius.

Recognizing her special talent for apprehensiveness—as she called the ability to get outside oneself and enter the creations of others—she chose the role of critic, "younger brother" to genius. She argued the virtue of her action for herself as well as for her readers while she was editor of *The Dial;* and in "A Dialogue," her brief dialectic between the critic and the creative artist in the guise of poet, she stated the rationale for the critic's existence and usefulness. He was to work as "a Seeker" side by side with the poet as "a Maker" to attain one and the same goal: an ideal standard of perfection that lay outside and beyond both.[1] Since to Margaret—as well as to Emerson, Parker, and others among the transcendentalists—the existence of the goal seemed only barely perceptible to most Americans, she did not underestimate the importance of the task that lay before the critic. It was nothing more or less than to help Americans—and American artists in particular—to equate literature with life and life with perfection.

In the manifesto of "The Editors to the Reader," which represented Emerson's reworking of Margaret's preliminary draft,
Emerson spoke for Margaret as well as for himself when he told
readers of *The Dial* politely but firmly that he intended to break
with convention and the past and to participate in the "protest
against usage" that the spirit of the present age demanded. To
this "protest" Margaret remained steadfastly dedicated to the
end of her life. She resolutely opposed the dead forms of the
past and demanded a fresh look at the progressive tendencies of
the age. By broadening the critic's function to include all aspects
of life—not just the literary or aesthetic—she helped to prepare
the way for Whitman and other modern writers who understood
that what counts in life also counts in literature.

I *The Critical Background*

It has already been shown that Margaret Fuller began to
study German literature and philosophy in the 1830's. Inspired
first by Carlyle to inquire into German authors, she undertook
to learn their language so that she could go directly to the
springs of their thought. In this undertaking she succeeded so
well that she was able not only to teach the language but also
to prepare respectable translations of Goethe and lesser German
writers. Although she planned carefully for an excursion into the
world of German philosophy by reading John Locke and several
exponents of the Scottish school of Common Sense, she soon
discovered that she possessed no bent for metaphysics.[2] Between
1836 and 1849, therefore, she channeled her energies into literature and art and into the social and political activities which she
believed were organically related to progress in all of the arts.
As she saw it, her function throughout these years was to interpret
European authors—and through them European culture—to her
fellow Americans because "this kind of culture would be precisely the counterpoise required by the utilitarian tendencies of
our day and place." [3]

A careful reading of Margaret's scattered and frequently ran-
dom comments concerning philosophy reveals that she never
systematically formulated a scientific basis for her chosen work.
But with the assistance of A. W. Schlegel, the German romantic
critic, and of Coleridge's exposition of Schlegel's organic theory,
and with the guidance of the writings of other nineteenth-century

thinkers, especially Goethe, she succeeded in developing a rather loose philosophical formulation. It approximated German idealism balanced by a strong sense of social ethics and a view of divinity that tended, at times, to be almost pantheistic. In her own temporized version of the chain of being, she saw the universe as an organic unit made up of interdependent parts in the process of becoming. Just as for Emerson "the worm mounts through all the spires of form," so for Margaret man must actively strive to interpret the laws of nature while aspiring to reach God, who remains transcendent in the present stage of human development.[4]

Her religious position was identical with that expressed in Emerson's "The Problem"; for she wrote: "I will not loathe sects, persuasions, systems, though I cannot abide in them one moment, for I see that by most men they are still needed. . . . I would learn from them all. . . . But let me set no limits from the past, to my own soul, or to any soul."[5] In these last words she was expressing sentiments which another Emersonian, Walt Whitman, would underline in "Passage to India," a statement of the same essential belief in eternal progress that motivated Margaret's critical outlook.

Again, like Emerson and Whitman, she rejected the Calvinistic conception of good and evil. For her, as well as for them, evil played no positive role in the divine plan; it was not an active force (part of an eternal dualism) but privative: "Evil is obstruction; Good is accomplishment."[6] Once and for all, she renounced New England Puritanism and its vision of a fallen mankind hedged about by sin and incapable of helping itself. On the foundation of ideas emanating from the Enlightenment and nourished by the romantic idealism of Germany, she planned to realize a new American Dream. In theological terms, she replaced the Puritan covenant of grace with a covenant of works—the only possible solution, she was convinced, for the problems of the free and independent citizens of an industrial democracy.

Like Gully Jimson, Joyce Cary's irrepressible son of Adam in *The Horse's Mouth*, Margaret believed that man had suffered a "Fall into freedom" instead of into sin. With freedom, man became responsible; and the burden of his responsibility involved work and more work—the curse of Adam. But by making his work creative, man could become truly human and achieve fulfillment as a rational, sentient being. The process would then be repeated in a cycle of creation and re-creation throughout an ever-ascending spiral. For Margaret, as well as for Gully Jimson, therefore, freedom could never depend simply on a lack of obstacles or restraint; it must be creation in the act. Margaret was under no illusions concerning this world of creation: "The artist's life is poor, sordid . . . the path does not open for him straight and clear in this our day." [7] Still, this was the direction in which salvation lay. For these reasons, though she often exhibited a generous humanitarianism, Margaret's literary and social criticism was always deeply rooted in humanism.

II *Theory and Practice*

During the quarter century immediately preceding Margaret Fuller's active participation in the cultural life of New England, criticism generally adhered to the conservative pattern laid down by the Scottish rhetoricians Lord Kames and Hugh Blair and supported by the school of Scottish realism. In Philadelphia, classicism and conservatism combined to keep the city's patrician atmosphere unchanged. New York produced no truly distinguished critics: only Bryant, a transplanted New Englander, showed any inclination to budge from tradition and to try new ideas. New England displayed some progress but its advance was slow. The analytic and judicial criticism inherited from the previous century gave way very gradually in magazines like the *North American Review*. In 1819, for example, Richard Henry Dana was forced to resign because of his intransigence in criticizing Pope and in praising Hazlitt.

There were some signs, however, that the old order was changing: in the mid-1830's Dana's Shakespearean criticism, the first American exposition of the Bard to show the influence of Schlegel and Coleridge, represented a completely fresh approach; and the welcome given to Frederick Henry Hedge and Dr. William Ellery Channing in the pages of the *The Christian Examiner* demonstrated that magazine's desire to soften the moralistic tone that had characterized its earlier pronouncements.[8]

When Margaret wrote "A Short Essay on Critics" for the first number of *The Dial*, she had already carefully thought out her theory of criticism, although her activity as a critic had been restricted up to that time to a youthful defense of Brutus, some

half-dozen articles for *The Western Messenger,* and her translator's preface to *Conversations with Goethe.* Drawing upon her
broad background reading in English and continental authors of
the eighteenth and nineteenth centuries, she had prepared a
"comprehensive" theory to replace the prevailing "subjective"
and "apprehensive" methods. She dismissed "subjective" critics as
simply reflexive because they gave the world nothing of "absolute, essential value" but only impressions of themselves. She
granted, however, some "ideal as well as historical value" to the
"apprehensive" or expressionistic critics because "they reproduce
the world of which they speak, and make it better known to us."
But only the "comprehensive" critic, she argued, could "enter the
nature of another being and judge his work by its own law";
only he "perceives the analogies of the universe, and how they
are regulated by an absolute, invariable principle." [9]

Once having affirmed belief in the existence of an organic unity
pervading the entire universe of forms, Margaret proceeded to
set down the qualifications of the critic who could read the
uniform hieroglyphic aright. He must share the temper of the
poet, the philosopher, and the trained observer: the poet's "eye
and sensitivity"; the philosopher's "spirit of inquiry" but not his
"hard-cemented masonry of method"; the "organic acuteness"
and "love of ideal perfection" of the keen observer whom mere
detail cannot blind. On the other hand, the critic must not think
himself infallible or seek to establish himself as leader of a
coterie. Nor should he prize "external consistency" or partisan-
ship so highly that he would reject "writings which wear the
distinctive traits of individual life." [10]

Summing up her protest against genteel criticism and coterie
wits, she expressed disdain for "the judicious man of the world"
and "his smooth sentences." She stated her preference for "some
earnest voice which is uttering thoughts, crude, rash, ill-arranged
it may be, but true to one human breast." [11] In essence her essay
amounted to a thorough disavowal of the basic principles followed by most of the American critics who had preceded her.
The critic as the watchdog of society; literature as a bulwark of
the status quo in religion, morals, and politics; literature as the
optimistic and rational exposition of proper society rather than
the voice of the individual (possibly pessimistic, mystical, or
agnostic)—all these ideas she either explicitly or implicitly denied
in her first full-fledged statement of critical purpose. [12]

In theory Margaret recognized two modes of criticism to match her dualistic conception of literature as the distillation of the mind of genius or as a means of communication among all peoples. She distinguished between one kind of critic who tries "by the highest standard of literary perfection . . . each work which comes in his way; rejecting all that is possible to reject, and reserving for toleration only what is capable of standing the severest test," and another who "enters into the natural history of everything . . . believes no impulse to be entirely in vain . . . and believes there is a beauty in each natural form, if its law and purpose be understood." [13] She saw possible dangers in both schools of thought: pedantry and hypercriticism in the first; sentimentality and genial indulgence in the second.

Ideally, she hoped for a golden age where the "highest sense of fulfilled excellence will be found to consist with the largest appreciation of every sign of life." [14] For the present in America, where "that soul that may shape her mature life scarce begins to know itself yet," she knew that the "genial and more affectionate" mode of criticism tended to prevail. [15] Genius was still rare, but she had no fear that it would stifle in an atmosphere that encouraged a more general expression of thought. She envisaged her proper function not only to include recognition of those who gave evidence of genius but also to extend encouragement to less talented writers of the people like William Thom and John Prince. [16] If she found Longfellow, Lowell, and Poe wanting, it was simply that she had measured them against an exacting ideal standard. While it is true that her measured praise for William Ellery Channing and Cornelius Mathews shows more than a little sentimentality, one should not overlook the fact that her criticism of them followed the organic or objective approach rather than the ideal.

Unlike many of her contemporaries, she did not fall into the trap of literary nationalism. On the one hand, her crusade against insularity took the direction of welcoming Irish immigrants and southern Europeans as sources of enrichment of the artistic life of America; on the other, it urged Americans to read the best among European authors but to write about what was deeply rooted in their own lives. As she put it: "The honey of Hymetus need not spoil the taste of the American wild bee, but only teach him not to content himself with the coarsest flowers when he might do better." Thus she used her knowledge of German folk ballads to encourage American writers to take a deeper interest in their own folklore, especially that of the vanishing Indian.[17] By emphasizing the native heritage and by encouraging her countrymen to strive for an organic expression of their age and its aspirations, she sought to work toward that harmony of the historical and ideal which she considered so necessary in criticism.

Alhough Margaret clearly perceived many of the important issues in aesthetics, she enjoyed considerably more success in literature in organizing and focusing her critical ideas than she did in the fine arts.[18] In her literary criticism, she more than once ran into conflict and contradictions when attempting to balance difficult equations like content versus form, the real versus the ideal, or representation versus expression; but she usually managed to find a solution that resulted in surprisingly just evaluations of literary works. Where the other arts were concerned, the results were not so happy. While her appraisals of Lowell, Poe, and Longfellow often went contrary to contemporary estimates and appear to be more in accordance with modern opinion, she never managed to transcend critical commonplace when discussing music, painting, or sculpture.

Her besetting fault appears to lie in her predilection for viewing all the arts in literary terms, a practice that resulted in blurring important distinctions among the various disciplines and thus prevented her from achieving the very comprehensiveness that she considered vital in the critic of stature. "What does the picture mean to say?" she asked while viewing Washington Allston's "Witch of Endor." And finding herself in disagreement with what she understood Allston's message to be, she labeled the painting unsatisfactory because it gave "no distinct impression." [19]

Since her theory of unity rested upon a concept of an organic succession of forms, she looked to each age to produce its own characteristic expression in art. For her own times, she considered that it was music. Beethoven seemed almost immortal to her: she prized his worship of truth, and in his music she heard the same romantic affirmation and prophecy of genius that she sought from poetry.[20] In her "Lives of the Great Composers," she wrote: "What the other arts indicate and philosophy infers, this all-enfolding language declares, nay publishes . . . that all truth is comprised in music and mathematics." [21]

Despite her efforts to evaluate music, Margaret's confusion of

conceptual with musical ideas—joined with an almost complete
disregard for the formal structure of musical compositions (witness her treatment of a technical treatise in *The Dial* [22])—leads
to the inescapable conclusion that she found music exciting and
sensuously stimulating but hardly a distinct art form obeying laws
and structural requirements of its own. For years she depended
upon it to sustain her during periods of loneliness or emotional
depression; her feeling for Beethoven was romanticism in its
purest form and measured the distance that separated her from
her other idol, Goethe, whose mastery and balance of mind and
heart, will and emotion, she was never able to achieve.

Even if the limitations under which the critic of the arts had
to labor in America in the 1830's and 1840's had been removed,
Margaret very likely would have failed to surmount her own
temperamental and philosophical weaknesses. True, before she
went to Europe to live, she had to depend largely on reading to
inform herself of the achievements in the different fields of art,
because the opportunities for listening to challenging and experi-
mental musical programs or for experiencing the world's master-
pieces of painting and sculpture were severely limited in New
England and New York. Her friendship with the musical critic,
John Dwight, and with painters like Allston and Christopher
Cranch was scarcely more rewarding aesthetically; for Allston's
career was largely behind him and Dwight's had hardly begun
when she knew them. Cranch was a good friend and companion,
but Margaret had little sympathy for his dilettante ways.

Restricted by these limited avenues of approach to the arts,
Margaret compounded her difficulties as a critic by relying on
her intuitions instead of following the standard she had learned
from Goethe: "To appreciate any man, learn first what object he
proposed to himself; next, what degree of earnestness he showed
with regard to attaining that object." Emerson did not immediately comprehend the degree of empathy that existed between
Margaret and artists in general, but he soon came to realize that
her taste in art was based on personal rather than on universal
grounds. "Her fancy and imagination were easily stimulated to
genial activity," he wrote, "and she erroneously thanked the artist
for the pleasing emotions and thoughts that rose in her mind."
Though Emerson was not always at his critical best when treating of Margaret, he spoke wisely this time—she was indeed an
enthusiast in the arts.

III *The Uses of Imagination*

Even the staunchest of Margaret's defenders would find it exceedingly difficult to overlook the faults of style that mar her written expression and weaken the effectiveness of some of her most important ideas. Several of the men who knew her well and who could speak from experience—Henry Hedge, James Clarke, Emerson, and Horace Greeley—considered her a graceful and effective conversationalist, whose spontaneity and wit produced finished and memorable sentences without any noticeable effort. But they also agreed that she left most of her gifts behind when she took up her pen. Only Edgar Allan Poe appears to have thought that there were no differences between her literary and conversational powers; and he is one of the most generous critics of her literary method and style, chiding her lightly for laxity of language and "excessive subjectiveness" but praising her forcefulness and boldness.[23]

Margaret was too honest with herself to be deluded for very long about her abilities as an author. After she had tried unsuccessfully to plan and write plays and short fiction, she recognized that she had no gift for creative prose. But since she believed strongly in her ideas and in her mission to communicate to others what she had learned about life, literature, and art, she continued to persevere with her expository writing. The Preface to her *Papers on Literature and Art* expresses her satisfaction that she had been able to accomplish so much. She says, "I have written enough, if what is afloat, and what lies hid in manuscript, were put together, to make a little library, quite large enough to exhaust the patience of the collector, if not of the reader."

Her "little library," as she calls it, contains some rather amazing items and exhibits. If one adds to it her extensive personal correspondence from abroad, her "Letters to the *Tribune*," and assigns a place for the lost manuscript of the revolution in Italy—which she hoped might become "a worthy chapter in the history of the world,"—the body of her writing begins to assume impressive proportions. Much of it, of course, displays the impatience with detail that prevented her, at times, from properly fleshing out the bones of her discourse and, at others, from cutting out the excessive description that hides and obscures her meaning. She often saw the principle that would unify what she was planning to write; but she was frequently prevented from achieving unity, either because she could not take the time to go through the steps necessary to reach it, or because she assumed, as she once remarked, "too much culture in the reader." Frequently she relied on her intuitions; and like most romantics, she was more successful in the flash of insight than she was in following through an extensive train of thought.

Both Hedge and Greeley had opportunity to watch Margaret at work, and they agree that she wrote with difficulty. Her slowness galled her because words came unbidden to her lips when she had someone "to call" her out, and she could not understand why she should be so unimaginative when she had to fashion her thoughts without an audience. Lydia Child told her that she seemed "to write with too much effort." [24] That there is much truth in this statement the following example will illustrate. Attempting to define woman's special genius, she writes rather cumbrously:

> More native is it to her to be the living model of the artist than to set apart from herself any one form in objective reality; more native to inspire and receive the poem, than to create it. In so far as soul is completely developed, all soul is the same; but in so far as it is modified in her as Woman, it flows, it breathes, it sings, rather than deposits soil, or finishes work; and that which is especially feminine flushes, in blossom, the face of earth, and pervades, like air and water, all this seeming globe, daily renewing and purifying its life.

Too often Margaret's writing appears to be under forced draft, as if she had wrung the life out of her ideas and then reported the lifeless remains from a sense of duty. She is at her best when her earnestness of thought shines through and overcomes her diffidence in style. Witness the conviction and sincerity of this passage about self-reliance and internal reform:

> Those who would reform the world must show that they do not speak in the heat of wild impulse; their lives must be unstained by passionate error; they must be severe lawgivers to themselves. They must be religious students of the divine purpose with regard to man, if they would not confound the fancies of the day with the requisitions of eternal good. Their liberty must be the liberty of law and knowledge.

She is at her worst when she is carried away by the extravagance and rhapsody that she learned from Jean Paul Richter or when she attempts to imitate the mystical outpourings and esoteric utterances of Novalis. Her sketch of the German poet Friedrich Klopstock, published in *The Dial* (January, 1841) but written some eight years earlier under the "magnetic" spell of Jean Paul, reveals these faults. In this speech of Meta, Klopstock's wife returned from the grave, Margaret's weakness for sentimentalizing is painfully evident:

> The thought of what thou must suffer convulsed my heart with one last pang. Once more I murmured the wish that I had so often expressed, that the sorrows of the survivor might have fallen to my lot rather than to thine. In that pang my soul extricated itself from the body, a sensation like that from exquisite fragrance came over me, and with breezy lightness I escaped into the pure serene. It was a moment of feeling wildly free and unobscured. I had not yet passed the verge of comparison. I could not embrace the infinite; and my joy was, like those of earth, intoxicating. Words cannot paint, even to thy eager soul, my friend, the winged swiftness, the glowing hopefulness of my path through the fields of azure.

Even in her summary of the argument of *Woman in the Nineteenth Century,* one place above all where she wished to be understood by her readers, she is guilty of figurative language that obscures rather than clarifies her thought. After referring to the growth of man as being "two-fold, masculine and feminine," she goes on to write:

> There can be no doubt that if these two developments were in perfect harmony, they would correspond to and fulfill one another like hemispheres, or the tenor and the bass in music.

> But there is no perfect harmony in human nature; and the two parts answer one another only now and then; or if there be a persistent consonance, it can only be traced at long intervals, instead of discoursing on an obvious melody.

Once she grew out of this habit of coloring her prose with obscure musical metaphors and murky images drawn from the romantic books that she favored during her immersion in the *Romantische-Schule,* her writing began to show decided improvement. Her articles in the *Tribune,* both during her sojourn in New York and after she had gone to Europe, are evidence that she could write a hard-hitting, concrete prose that contained enough "graphicality" to satisfy even Poe, who dreamed up the word. In one of her letters to the *Tribune* from abroad, for example, she paints a masterly word picture of one of the three types of American tourist whom she had encountered in Europe.

> Then there is the conceited American, instinctively bristling and proud of—he knows not what. He does not see, not he, that the history of humanity for many centuries is likely to have produced results it requires some training, some devotion, to appreciate and profit by. With his great clumsy hands, only fitted to work on a steam engine, he seizes the old Cremona violin, makes it shriek with anguish in his grasp, and then declares he thought it was all humbug before he came and now he knows it; that there is not really any music in these old things; that the frogs in one of our swamps make much finer, for they are young and alive. To him the etiquettes of courts and camps, the ritual of the Church, seem simply silly—and no wonder, profoundly ignorant as he is of their origin and meaning.

If the reader allows for the difficulties presented by Margaret's sometimes obscure and sometimes almost unreadable prose style—and unless he is willing to make this allowance for every one of the transcendental writers, he might as well write them off as a nearly total loss—he will find considerable value in what she wrote. Despite the haphazard arrangement of the edited version of her letters, diaries, and journals in the *Memoirs*, the record of her spiritual and emotional conflicts in attempting to reconcile the poles of thought between which she and the other transcendentalists uneasily ranged is an invaluable introduction to the New England mind in the early nineteenth century. Though not settling completely the problem that bothered most New Englanders—how to reconcile Goethe's undeniable genius and just as undeniable immorality with the standards of Puritan other-worldliness—her essays on Goethe in *The Dial* did much to make known to her countrymen the personality of the great man by changing the grounds for evaluating his conduct. In so far as she was able to show the men and women of New England that Goethe should be judged by the law of his own genius, she was also helping them to realize that they must be true to their own hearts and minds instead of submitting their souls to some tribunal of social conformity.

Her first original book, *Summer on the Lakes*, is, in part, one of the curiosities of literature, with its digressions and transgressions against the canons of good travel literature. But it is also, as Poe was acute to perceive, an irreplaceable record of impressions by an intelligent and sensitive Eastern visitor of a developing frontier that few Americans ever bothered to look at. While the book contains waste and arid regions, it is also graced with some of Margaret's most felicitous observations.

In the advice of "The Book to the Reader"—located in a somewhat unusual position at the end of her book—Margaret invited readers to partake of "a dish of homely sweets" and to visit "in the places where the berries grow, [where] a sweeter fruit the ready sense commands." By so doing she suggested that she had allied herself with the realistic contingent of travel writers rather than with those who took the high road of Romance. Unlike Charles Dickens, whose *American Notes* had recently demonstrated how *not* to see a new country, Margaret was determined to give an accurate account of the scenes that she had visited. For this reason she based her book closely on the journal that she had kept religiously during her journey, adding to her travel notes only where the fruits of her research helped to amplify an on-the-spot observation.

Her most serious violation of unity resulted from the insertion of a lengthy account of Justinus Kerner's *Seherin von Prevorst*, a report of some pseudo-scientific investigations of spiritualistic phenomena. The inclusion of "Mariana," a semi-autobiographical story of schooldays, was hardly less distracting. The result was a volume *sui generis*, although in form it is somewhat reminiscent of Heine's famous *Reisebilder* (familiar to every armchair traveler in the first generation of American transcendentalists); and, in spirit and design, her book looks forward to Henry David Thoreau's *A Week on the Concord and Merrimack Rivers*.

Her growing curiosity about a region to which her Uncle William and several of her friends had moved, and which was daily helping to depopulate New England, increased Margaret's desire to discover and publicize the significance of this new migration. The following passage, which defines the spirit with which she undertook her pilgrimage, expresses both her purpose for traveling and for making a book out of her travels:

> I come to the West prepared for the distaste I must experience at its mushroom growth. I know that where "go ahead" is the only motto, the village cannot grow into the gentle proportions that successive lives and the gradations of experience involun-

tarily give. . . . The march of peaceful is scarcely less wanton than that of warlike invasion. The old landmarks are broken down, and the land for a season bears none, except of the rudeness of conquest and the needs of the day . . . I have come prepared to see all this, to dislike it, but not with stupid narrowness to distrust or defame. On the contrary, while I will not be so obliging as to confound ugliness with beauty, discord with harmony, and laud and be contented with all I meet, when it conflicts with my best desires and tastes, I trust by reverent faith to woo the mighty meaning of the scene, perhaps to foresee the law by which a new order, a new poetry, is to be evoked from this chaos. . . .

Summer on the Lakes begins at Niagara, where the author's mood of "quiet satisfaction," born of finding, at first, the reality of the Falls close to her preconceived notions of it, quickly changes to a feeling of "undefined dread" as the "perpetual trampling of the waters" seizes her senses. Shaken out of her literary approach to the new and overpowering scenes around her, Margaret then begins to keep truer faith with her readers. From this point on, her writing shows an increasing awareness of the spirit of place; people and events come alive before the readers' eyes as she gazes upon the world of the pioneer candidly and perceptively.

Nothing in Margaret's previous experience had prepared her for the sense of freedom and expansiveness that she began to feel as she and her companions traveled by boat to Chicago. But she was somewhat disheartened by the failure of other travelers to realize the import of their new prospects. "The people on the boat were almost all New Englanders seeking their fortunes," she writes. "They had brought with them their habits of calculation, their cautious manners, their love of polemics. It grieved me to hear these immigrants, who were to be the fathers of a new race, all, from the old man down to the little girl, talking not of what they should do, but of what they should get in the new scene." As her book clearly illustrates, she took increasing pains henceforth to keep the reader fully informed of the new relationships between the people and their frontier environment.

Arrived in Chicago, Margaret at first sight found the rolling prairie land "the very desolation of dullness." But the excitement of the vast panorama spread out before her soon overcame her:

"I would ascend the roof of the house where we lived and pass many hours, needing no sight but the moon reigning in the heavens or starlight falling upon the lake, until all the lights were out in the island grove of men beneath my feet, and felt that nearer heaven there was nothing but this lovely, still reception on the earth; no towering mountains, no deep tree-shadows, nothing but plain earth and water bathed in light."

Her next experience, an excursion of three weeks through northern Illinois with Sarah Clarke and Sarah's brother William as a guide, provided a splendid opportunity to fill her book with poetic impressions of the "Western Eden" into which she had come. But her hackneyed description of "the stately thickets, with their pathways green" leaves the imagination untouched. However, her pithy comment on civilization's course sticks in the memory: "Wherever the hog comes, the rattlesnake disappears, the omnivorous traveler safe in its stupidity, willingly and easily makes a meal of the most dangerous of reptiles and one which the Indian looks on with mystic awe. Even so the white settler pursues the Indian and is victor in the chase."

In similar fashion, she enlivens her brief narrative of sharing the crude hospitality of a crowded prairie tavern with a humourous account of an Englishwoman who found the prospect of sleeping in the bar-room beneath her dignity and who sat up all night, "wrapped in her blanket-shawl and with a neat lace cap upon her head—so that she would have looked perfectly the lady if anyone had come in—shuddering and listening. She watched as her parent country watches the seas, that nobody may do wrong in any case, and deserved to have met some interruption, she was so well prepared. However, there was none, other than from the nearness of some twenty sets of powerful lungs." Anecdotes like these appealed to Horace Greeley when he read the book and led him to say, "I still consider 'Summer on the Lakes' unequalled, especially in its pictures of the Prairies and of the sunnier aspects of Pioneer life." [25]

Since Margaret was not trying to prepare a Baedeker for the reader—an outline of geography being incidental to her main purpose of giving the flavor of her experiences—*Summer on the Lakes* lacks systematic arrangement. Its only order is a loose kind of chronology, and its form shows the episodic qualities of the journal upon which it is based. While she was traveling by wagon throughout the sparsely settled rural areas of Illinois or journeying into the even less populous and wilder areas of the Wisconsin territory, she kept no diary but trusted to memory to recall later her reactions to local manners and customs, and she relied upon her good judgment to evaluate the effects of pioneering upon transplanted Easterners. Thus her comments on the imitativeness of settlers and on their failure to take advantage of the opportunities offered by a spacious and uncluttered land still free from burdensome traditions ring with spontaneity and sparkle with the charm of fresh observation. They easily outrival in literary force the somewhat bookish remarks and more studied comments that she makes when she returns to Chicago. There, in the growing metropolis, as though civilization has already reclaimed her as an errant child, she drops into a philosophic mood in which she speculates concerning the need of a type of man "religious, virtuous, and sagacious; a man of universal sympathies, but self possessed," who will be equal to the greatness of America. The idea is sound, but it tends to be imposed upon experience rather than to grow out of it.

Again, she vitiates her account of a visit to the Island of Mackinaw and of subsequent experiences among the Chippewa and Ottawa tribes encamped there, by citing bookish authorities and by interspersing literary allusions among penetrating comments about Indian life and character based on her own firsthand observation. Still forcing her writing at times into stilted diction and tortuous sentence structure—almost as though she lacked confidence in her own insights or felt at ease only when she could support them with her considerable baggage of learning and allusion—she all too frequently distracts the reader whose attention had initially been seized and then held by her keen and appropriate comment.

Still, if one makes allowance for the sentimental touches resulting from Margaret's acquaintance with previous travel writers like Anna Jameson or from her having fallen too deeply under the spell of Sir Walter Scott, whose presence she sincerely thought was needed to catch the true spirit of the dusky Indian tribesmen and their squaws, he will receive considerable benefit and pleasure from what is undeniably a perceptive and often charming recital of people and events by a traveler upon whom nothing significant is ever lost.

When it was first published, Margaret's little book received a warm reception from her close friends and acquaintances; but the general public never showed enough interest in it to warrant a second edition. Its only reprinting came as a result of Arthur Fuller's edition of her writings in *At Home and Abroad.* Even at that, she fared better at the time than did Thoreau some five years later when he tried to interest the reading public in *A Week on the Concord and Merrimack Rivers.* Posterity has seen fit to rescue Thoreau's work, but *Summer on the Lakes* remains a relatively obscure piece of Americana.

Much better known, of course, is *Woman in the Nineteenth Century,* although its reputation comes not so much from the reader's first-hand acquaintance with its contents or from Margaret's more successful command of language or logic, but from her defense of basic human rights and her illustration of "the eternal feminine" in women from ancient history, mythology, and Goethe's gallery of heroines. To paraphrase its argument is to restate the entire philosophy of organic unity and succession of forms that constitutes the basic belief of Margaret Fuller: the effort to unravel the thread of its sometimes labyrinthine ways is most worth-while.

The earliest printed version of Margaret's theses regarding women appeared as the lead article in *The Dial* of July, 1843, under the title of "The Great Lawsuit.—Man *versus* Men; Woman *versus* Women." Encouraged by the response to her views, Margaret decided to expand her article and prepare it for publication in book form. When it was finally ready for the press late in the fall of the following year, she had changed her title—in response to urging from friends—to the more general *Woman in the Nineteenth Century,* although she still preferred the more cumbersome, legalistic label as being a better description of the contents of the book. It was the first formal statement of feminism to be prepared by an American; only Mary Wollstonecraft's *Vindication of the Rights of Woman* (1792) preceded it.

Although there was much in common in the lives of the Englishwoman and Margaret Fuller, their books reveal a difference in emphasis that is largely the result of contrasts in the intellectual climate of their respective ages. In Margaret's time, the doctrines of socialism had supplanted the concept of abstract rights that preoccupied the circle of Miss Wollstonecraft, William Godwin, and Thomas Paine. The gospel preached by Fourier had replaced the earlier theory of natural rights espoused by Rousseau and his disciples. In her pioneer work, Margaret used key concepts borrowed from the French socialist to bolster her defense of improved conditions for her sex. As she begins her work, she writes boldly, "I solicit of women that they will lay it to heart to ascertain what is for them the liberty of law." Later, nearing her conclusion, she urges that women be given the opportunity to choose their own occupations. "Let them be Sea-Captains, if you will," she exclaims. Both these principles— "liberty of law" and "attractive industry"—were prominent features of the Fourieristic system.

In the Preface, dated November, 1844, Margaret states the central thesis of her book:

> . . . while it is the destiny of Man, in the course of the ages, to ascertain and fulfill the law of his being . . . the action of prejudices and passions which attend, in the day, the growth of the individual, is continually obstructing the holy work that is to make the earth a part of heaven. By Man I mean both man and woman; these are the two halves of one thought. I lay no especial stress on the welfare of either. I believe that the development of the one cannot be effected without that of the other. My highest wish is that this truth should be distinctly and rationally apprehended and the condition of life and of freedom recognized as the same for the daughters and sons of time; twin exponents of a divine thought.

This parallelism is never systematically developed in the book; yet Margaret is remarkably objective in dealing with her subject. As she indicates in her two epigraphs—"Frailty, thy name is Woman" and "The Earth waits for her Queen"—she considers women's willingness to be subservient to men partially responsible for the continuing restrictions upon their activities. If this weakness is to be overcome, she argues, women must be allowed to develop according to their own natures.

Like Thoreau in *Walden,* Margaret sets out to investigate—to find a lowest common denominator for living—and then to recommend a program of self-reliance:

> Ascertain the true destiny of Woman; give her legitimate hopes and a standard within herself; marriage and all other relations . . . [will] by degrees be harmonized with these. . . . What woman needs is not as a woman to act or rule, but as a nature to grow, as an intellect to discern, as a soul to live freely and unimpeded, to unfold such powers as were given her when we left our common home.

Margaret observes that self-reliance is unfortunately considered a fault in most women. "They are taught to learn their rule from without," she adds, "not to unfold it from within. . . . The difficulty is to get them to the point from which they shall naturally develop self-respect, and learn self-help."

Having stated her purpose and suggested a workable method for promoting human welfare, Margaret then proceeds to range widely through history and literature for evidence to support her contentions. She illustrates her argument by references to mythology, classical literature, and ancient and modern history; she also buttresses her concepts with quotations and examples from the work of leading contemporary thinkers and writers. She concludes that, as far as women are concerned, a turning point has finally been reached in human history. "The time is come when Eurydice is to call for an Orpheus, rather than Orpheus for Eurydice," she writes. And in America, she continues, a beginning appears likely to be made; for "this country is as surely destined to elucidate a great moral law, as Europe was to promote the mental culture of man." She cites the work of abolitionism—and especially the role of women in it—as a case in point.

"Man is not willingly ungenerous," Margaret declares. "He wants faith and love, because he is not yet himself an elevated being." He needs a sign; but when it is given, he offers not merely approval but homage to womanly virtue. From Egyptian and Mosaic law, the legends of Greece and Rome, the plays of Shakespeare and the verse of Spenser, the histories of Isabella of Spain and Elizabeth of England, and the literary accounts of Italian and German reverence for womanhood, Margaret chose examples to support her statement that men are capable of recognizing the true worth of women. For the most part, she sticks to the narrow and undeviating path of unity and logic, but occasionally she allows herself to be diverted by an unusual character or by a stirring incident. Such is the result when she undertakes to tell the story of King Cyrus and his captive Panthea, the wife of Abradatus. The tale is one of nobility and great sacrifice, but it is related at considerable length and at the expense of the reader's interest in the larger story that she is trying to narrate.

In cultures where men have raised themselves sufficiently

above poverty and ignorance to appreciate natural beauty and human values, women have never lacked for power, Margaret declares. But unless vanity overcomes wisdom, she adds, women do not seek power or wealth or authority over men. What women want is simply "the birthright of every being capable of receiving it,—the freedom, the religious, the intelligent freedom of the universe to use its means, to learn its secret, as far as Nature has enabled them, with God alone for their guide and their judge." It is simply not true, she concludes, that any woman, properly enlightened concerning her nature and its potential development, would ever wish to be a man or to usurp man's prerogatives.

Women like Mary Wollstonecraft and George Sand—and perhaps she toyed with the idea of including herself—impressed Margaret as falling into a special category. She writes: "Such beings as these, rich in genius, of most tender sympathies, capable of high virtue and a chastened harmony, ought not to find themselves, by birth, in a place so narrow, that, in breaking bonds, they become outlaws." But there is danger, she admits, in overvaluing either sensibility or intellect. "A being of infinite scope must not be treated with an exclusive view to any one relation," she cautions. "The intellect, no more than the sense of hearing, is to be cultivated merely not that Woman may be a more valuable companion to Man, but because the Power who gave a power, by its mere existence signifies that it must be brought out toward perfection."

With a frankness that shocked her contemporaries, Margaret was broadly critical of the institution of marriage as it functioned in her day, and she dared to speak openly about the evils of prostitution. Expressing her admiration for Mrs. Jameson's courage in protesting against the double standard, Margaret censures, with all the disdain at her command, the "legislator and man of the world" who argue that prostitution is a "necessary accompaniment of *civilization*." The European marriage *de convenance* impressed her as being no better than the morality of the Turkish slave-harem.

She identifies four types of marriage: the household partnership, a union of mutual idolatry, intellectual companionship, and the religious marriage. But only the last type—which embraces household wisdom, respect for one's partner, intellectual communion, and devotion to an unselfish ideal—fully qualifies as a satisfactory and lasting union as far as she is concerned. Actually, she puts much of her own feeling and experience into her book. Miranda, like Mariana in *Summer on the Lakes,* is a thinly veiled portrait of herself; and in her rather passionate defense of old maids, there is an element of special pleading, just as her remarks concerning the failure of society to bring out fairly "the electrical, the magnetic element in Woman" refer to her own highly charged and intuitive personality. In what constitutes almost a general judgment of her life at the moment of writing, she states: "Women who combine this organization with creative genius are very commonly unhappy at present."

Casting about for male authorities to buttress her arguments on behalf of women, Margaret settled upon three men whom she called "prophets of the coming age." In Emanuel Swedenborg, whom she considered a balance between the scientific and the poetic, she discerned a man whose ideas of marriage were satisfactory and whose thoughts about women placed no obstacles in the path of their progress. Though his philosophy resembled Quakerism, which she also admired, she preferred it because it appeared to her to be broader in scope. She held certain reservations about the materialism of Charles Fourier, believing him to be somewhat superficial and "fixed on the outward more than the inward needs of Man"; but she admired his faith in individual growth and found his views on equality of the sexes satisfactory. Goethe came closest, however, to approximating her ideal. Her admiration for the different types of feminine temperament displayed in *Wilhelm Meister* was unqualified, and Goethe's doctrine of self-culture completely satisfied her. "He aims at a pure self-subsistence," she writes with pleasure, "and a free development of any powers with which they [women] may be gifted by nature as much for them as for men. They are units addressed as souls." With Goethe, she held that character must be built from within; with Fourier, she was equally convinced that institutions must be strengthened from without.

Closer to Margaret in many respects than these three thinkers was Dr. William Ellery Channing, whose death in 1842 had been a great loss to her. In her book, she pays him a rich and well-deserved tribute; but no words of commendation can equal the less voluble but still more impressive expression of gratitude implied in her continued emphasis upon Channing's doctrine of the importance of the human soul; upon his defense of self-culture and the purity and lofty purpose of women; upon his indignation at all forms of religious, political, and social injustice; and finally upon his firmly held belief that America was to produce a new and higher moral law.

Margaret attached no particular importance to women's political rights; she simply included them when she appealed to man to remove all "arbitrary barriers" to the development of his twin in creation. She asks man to make woman free even as he is free and to confer upon woman all the privileges that he has gained for himself. In her wildest imaginings, Margaret never expected woman to be given immediately the liberty for which her book was asking. But even if the improbable were to happen and women were to be suddenly enfranchised, she felt confident that their inborn sense of decorum and their love of moderation would prevent them from abusing their privileges.

Horace Greeley published *Woman in the Nineteenth Century* in February, 1845. Offered at fifty cents a copy, the whole edition was sold within a week of publication; and Margaret received eighty-five dollars for her efforts. Reaction to her tract for the times was strong and mixed. Anger was expressed in several quarters because of her request for legal and political equality. The *Broadway Journal* attacked her personally: "Her most direct writing is on a subject no virtuous woman can treat justly. No woman is a true woman who is not wife and mother." Avoiding personalities, William Cullen Bryant, the editor of *The Evening Post*, stuck to the facts: "although its language is pretty strong, the thoughts it puts forth are so important that we should rejoice to know it read by every man and woman in America."

The clamor over Margaret's book gradually subsided, but its fame spread rapidly throughout America and abroad. When the women's rights conventions were held in the early 1850's, it was frequently cited by participants as the source from which they had derived the courage to fight for their rights. Nearly forty years after its appearance, Julia Ward Howe wrote: "Nothing that has been written or said in later days, has made its teaching superfluous." [26] When the supporters of women's rights began to concentrate their efforts on suffrage, interest in Margaret's work began to wane; in the world of the twentieth century, a more pragmatic audience, interested in concrete causes and direct action, has almost entirely forgotten the book that established the philosophic basis for the freedoms presently enjoyed by women.

IV   *The Poet*

Margaret Fuller never really considered herself seriously as a poet. In an age when lisping in numbers was taken for granted, she was self-critical enough to feel bad because she lacked poetic fire. Of the poems in her journal, she wrote, "I am ashamed when I think there is scarce a line of poetry in them. All 'rhetorical and impassioned' as Goethe said of Mme de Stael." [27] Like Emily Dickinson, Margaret often sent her friends verse bouquets to accompany the flowers that she picked from her garden for them. But her poetic nosegays reveal none of the daring use of language that makes Emily's thought seem so delightfully spontaneous. "To ——, with Heartsease" is characteristic of Margaret:

> Content, in purple lustre clad,
> Kingly serene, and golden glad,
> No demi-hues of sad contrition,
> No pallors of enforced submission;—
> Give me such content as this.
> And keep awhile the rosy bliss.

Just as much as Emerson, Margaret believed that "All thinking is analogizing, and it is the use of life to learn metonymy." [28] But the collection of poems in the volume *Life Without and Life Within* proves that she possessed neither the imagination nor control of symbols necessary for the poetic function. Henry Hedge's statement that "much of the poetry that is produced in this age is a mere accident of the age and has no root in the soul" explains part of what is wrong with Margaret's verse. Emerson supplies the rest of the explanation: "A poem should not need its relation to life to explain it; it should be a new life, not still half engaged in the soil, like the new created lions in Eden." [29]

V   *The Flux of Time*

Margaret Fuller still casts a long shadow. Commenting on a recent publication by a modern essayist, the book reviewer for the New York *Times* quotes the author as drawing a parallel between Mary McCarthy and Margaret. He then goes on to suggest that the author herself "shares Mary McCarthy's brilliance, Margaret Fuller's masterly range of ideas and Virginia Woolf's aloof felicities of style." [30] Margaret's image begins to come into perspective. But another reviewer in the current issue of one of America's leading magazines of opinion culls from *The Letters of Oscar Wilde* (1962) a reference to what he calls Wilde's "delightful remarks on the American blue-stocking, Margaret Fuller, 'to whom Venus gave everything except beauty, and Pallas everything except wisdom.'" [31] Once again the image is blurred and distorted; the cult of personality has superseded the record of achievement, and a quip takes the place of criticism.

The memory of Margaret Fuller deserves fairer assessment. Her personal influence on the men and women who shared with her the spiritual revolution of the "Transcendental" period; her efforts, as teacher, translator, editor, author, journalist, freedom fighter, and historian, to bring about a cross-fertilization of American and European cultures; her campaign to overcome the parochialism and provincialism of her fellow Americans and to replace them with the broader viewpoint of internationalism— these constitute the evidence on which any responsible evaluation of her career must be based. The curtains of history should never be allowed to close on the flesh-and-blood woman who left this remarkable record behind her; despite the flux of time, her life remains a challenge and an inspiration to all who prize a willing heart and a rebellious spirit.

Notes and References

Chapter One

1. Manuscript, Fuller Papers, Vol. I, Houghton Library.
2. *Memoirs of Margaret Fuller Ossoli,* ed. by R. W. Emerson, W. H. Channing, and J. F. Clarke (Boston, 1852), I, 133.
3. MS letter from Timothy Fuller, dated April 13, 1820, Fuller Papers, Vol. IX, Houghton Library. Letter from Margaret to her father, dated Jan. 16, 1820, is evidence of her deep love for him.
4. See Arthur B. Fuller, *Historical Notices of Thomas Fuller and His Descendants with a Genealogy of the Fuller Family 1638-1902* (Cambridge, 1902). End papers in Madeleine Stern's *The Life of Margaret Fuller* (New York, 1942) contain genealogical charts of Fuller ancestry.
5. See *Memoirs,* I, 14-16. Psychological analysis leaning toward Freudian interpretation given in Katherine Anthony's *Margaret Fuller* (New York, 1920), pp. 16-26.
6. *Memoirs,* I, 20.
7. *Ibid.,* I, 127. See also article by René Wellek, "The Minor Transcendentalists and German Philosophy," *NEQ,* XV (December, 1942), 677-79.
8. See review entitled "French Novelists of the Day," New York *Daily Tribune,* Feb. 1, 1845. Reprinted in *Life Without and Life Within,* ed. by A. B. Fuller (New York, 1869), pp. 158-68; also in *The Writings of Margaret Fuller,* ed. by Mason Wade (New York, 1941), pp. 301-11.
9. "Cinders from the Ashes," *Atlantic Monthly,* XXIII (January, 1869), 116, 117.
10. Letter dated, March 5, 1826, in *Memoirs,* I, 55.
11. For an account of Bancroft and Hedge's European experiences, see Orie W. Long's *Literary Pioneers* (Cambridge, Mass., 1935), pp. 108-59. See also Long's *Frederick Henry Hedge: A Cosmopolitan Scholar* (Portland, 1940). Hedge's remarks on Margaret are printed in *Memoirs,* I, 90-96.
12. Manuscript in Fuller Papers, Boston Public Library. Partially reprinted, with names omitted, in *Memoirs,* I, 283, and Thomas W. Higginson's *Margaret Fuller Ossoli* (Boston, 1887), p. 37.
13. See *The Letters of James Freeman Clarke to Margaret Fuller,* ed. by John W. Thomas (Hamburg, 1957).
14. Letter from Clarke, dated May 6, 1834, *ibid.,* p. 75.

15. *Memoirs*, I, 139-40.

16. For Goethe's influence, see Frederick A. Braun, *Margaret Fuller and Goethe* (New York, 1910). Claims that Margaret Fuller was the first American to see the world-poet as an ethical leader and to understand his mission to humanity in this light. *Ibid.*, p. 214.

17. *Memoirs*, I, 121-22.

18. MS letter, dated March 6, 1835, in Fuller Papers, Boston Public Library. Reprinted in part in Higginson, *op. cit.*, p. 48.

19. *Memoirs*, I, 128.

20. Manuscript journal (1833) in Fuller Papers, Houghton Library.

21. For life of Ward, see George W. Cooke, *An Historical and Biographical Introduction to Accompany The Dial* (New York, 1961), pp. 36-40. See also Ralph W. Emerson, *Letters to a Friend 1838-1853*, ed. by Charles E. Norton (Boston, 1899) and Barker-Ward Papers, Houghton Library.

22. For her criticisms of American life, see *Society in America* (1837) and *Retrospect of Western Travel* (1838).

23. See Alexander E. Jones, "Margaret Fuller's Attempt to Write Fiction," *The Boston Public Library Quarterly*, VI (April, 1954), 67-73.

24. James Clarke's letters from Louisville, dated Sept. 15 and Oct. 4, 1835, deal with his role in leaking details of story. See Thomas, *Letters*.

25. *Memoirs*, I, 154.

Chapter Two

1. Margaret did much more than contribute a few articles to the *Western Messenger*. She urged men like Henry Hedge and Professor Farrar to write for it; and she continued to give strong moral support to Clarke, whose letters prove how much he depended on her for encouragement and intellectual excitement. See Thomas, *Letters*, p. 75f., especially letter dated Sept. 8, 1834.

2. See letters dated Feb. 20, March 16, April 12, 1835, in Thomas, *op. cit.*

3. *Ibid.*, pp. 94-95.

4. Letter dated March 17, 1836, *Memoirs*, I, 166.

5. Letter dated Feb. 26, 1836, Thomas, *op. cit.*, p. 115.

6. MS letter dated Oct. 6, 1834, in Fuller Papers, Houghton Library.

7. MS letter dated Feb. 1, 1835, in Fuller Papers, Houghton Library.

8. Quoted in *Memoirs*, I, 153.

9. *Memoirs*, I, 202.

10. MS letter, dated August 8, 1836, in Emerson Papers, Houghton Library. Reprinted in Rusk, *Letters*, II, 32.

11. *Memoirs*, I, 172.

12. Alcott's early acquaintance with Margaret Fuller can easily be traced in the entries of his unpublished diary, Fuller Papers, Boston Public Library. Several comments are reprinted in *Memoirs*, I, 172.

13. See Letter from Emerson dated October 20, 1836, in Emerson Papers, Houghton Library. Reprinted in Rusk, *Letters*, II, 41.

14. *Memoirs*, I, 175,.

15. MS letter in Fuller Papers, Houghton Library. Reprinted in Wade, *Writings*, pp. 547-48.

16. MS Letter to Hedge, dated April 6, 1837, in Fuller Papers, Houghton Library. Reprinted partially in Wade, *Writings*, pp. 547-48, and partially in Higginson, *Margaret Fuller*, p. 78.

17. Letter dated April 11, 1837, in Emerson Papers, Houghton Library. Copy in Fuller Papers, Boston Public Library.

18. MS letter dated June 27, 1837, in Fuller Papers, Boston Public Library.

19. She evidently used opium to relieve her pain because Emerson, in a postscript to his letter of June 16, 1837, conveys his wife's message to "abhor opium, which as a reasonable woman you must and will do." See Rusk, *Letters*, II, 82.

20. Letter dated August 14, 1837, printed in Higginson, *Margaret Fuller*, p. 87. Copy in Fuller Papers, Boston Public Library.

21. Manuscript, Fuller Papers, Boston Public Library. Printed in *Memoirs*, I, 183.

22. Letter dated July 8, 1837, reprinted in Higginson, *Margaret Fuller*, p. 81.

23. MS Letter dated July 18, 1837, in Emerson Papers, Houghton Library. Reprinted in Rusk, *Letters*, p. 88. Paraphrase in *Journals*, IV, 256-57.

24. Quoted in *Memoirs*, I, 230.

25. *Ibid.*, p. 195.

26. MS letter, dated August 14, 1837, in Fuller Papers, Boston Public Library.

27. See May 4, 1837, entry in *Journals*, IV, 225.

28. MS Letter dated Nov. 16, 1837, at Providence, in Fuller Papers, Houghton Library.

29. See MS letter to Newcomb, dated Feb. 24, 1840, in Fuller Papers, Houghton Library.

30. Manuscript in Fuller Papers, Boston Public Library. Reprinted in *Memoirs*, I, 186.

31. *Ibid.*, I, 189.

32. Emerson, *Journals*, IV, 333. Entry is dated Oct. 20, 1837.

33. The *Memoirs* contain only hints of Margaret's attachment.

Ward was supposed to be one of the authors, but he withdrew in favor of James Clarke. See MS letter to Sarah Ward dated Oct. 15, 1839, for Margaret's reaction to Sam Ward's thinking of her as a mother.

34. See manuscripts in Fuller Papers, Boston Public Library. With minor omissions and some changing around, these remarks are printed in *Memoirs*, I, 189.

35. MS letter dated May 24, 1838, Emerson Papers, Houghton Library. Reprinted in Rusk, *Letters*, II, 135.

36. See Thomas, *Letters*, for letter dated May 21, 1838.

37. MS letter dated June 28, 1838, in Emerson Papers, Houghton Library. Reprinted in Rusk, *Letters*, II, 142.

38. MS letter dated March 1, 1838, in Fuller Papers, Boston Public Library. Reprinted in Higginson, *Margaret Fuller*, p. 90.

39. See her own comments about teaching in *Memoirs*, I, 178-80. Also Harriet Johnson, "Margaret Fuller as Known by her Scholars," *The Christian Register* (April 21, 1910), pp. 426-29; Henry Greene, "The Greene-St. School and Its Teachers," *Publications of the Rhode Island Historical Society* (1898).

40. Letter dated Nov. 8, 1838, in Higginson, *Margaret Fuller*, p. 92.

41. Letter dated Dec. 9, 1838, *ibid.*, p. 94.

Chapter Three

1. For Norton's remarks, see *The Transcendentalists*, edited by Perry Miller (Cambridge, 1950), pp. 193-96.

2. Follen was Clarke's teacher and a close friend of Dr. Channing. He undoubtedly played an influential role in disseminating German thought in New England because he was for some time the only real authority on the language who could advise "readers" like Clarke, Margaret Fuller, Channing, and Emerson. See *The Works of Charles Follen with a Memoir of His Life* (Boston, 1841), 5 vols. Also article on Follen's "Inaugural Address' in *Christian Examiner*, XI (January, 1832), 373-80.

3. *Memoirs*, I, 234.

4. Part of summary of her argument of *Woman in the Nineteenth Century* (Boston, 1855), pp. 168-69. Reprinted in Wade, *Whetstone of Genius*, p. 289.

5. For outline of her plans to bring German literature to the American public, see *Memoirs*, I, 168-69.

6. "The Transcendentalist" in *The Complete Essays and Other Writings* (New York: Modern Library; 1950), pp. 87, 90, 92-93.

7. *Memoirs*, II, 85. Her distinction between faith and under-

standing appears to be borrowed from Carlyle's interpretation of Kant.

8. Quoted in *Memoirs*, II, 26-27, 28, 29.

9. Letter to Caroline Sturgis dated March 9, 1839, reprinted in Wade, *Writings*, p. 552. This lengthy letter gives a clear picture of Margaret's state of mind while she was "resting up" in Groton.

10. Copy by Emerson of partial contents of letter dated Jan. 7, 1839, in Emerson Papers, Houghton Library. Reprinted in Rusk, *Letters*, II, 178. Rest of letter reprinted in Higginson, *Margaret Fuller*, p. 95.

11. MS letter to Margaret dated March 8, 1839, in Emerson Papers, Houghton Library. Reprinted in Rusk, *Letters*, II, 191.

12. MS letter dated March 4, 1839, in Fuller Papers, Boston Public Library. Reprinted in Rusk, *ibid.*, pp. 191-92. See reprint of Very's comments on Hamlet in Miller, *The Transcendentalists*, pp. 353-56.

13. MS diary in Fuller Papers, Boston Public Library.

14. MS letter dated June 7, 1839, in Emerson Papers, Houghton Library. Reprinted in Rusk, *Letters*, II, 203.

15. Higginson, *Margaret Fuller*, p. 189.

16. Journal entry in O. B. Frothingham, *Theodore Parker* (Boston, 1874), p. 140.

17. MS letter in Fuller Papers, Houghton Library. Reprinted in *Memoirs*, I, 324-28.

18. *Ibid.*, p. 325.

19. *Memoirs*, I, 266-67.

20. *Ibid.*, p. 308.

21. "Margaret Fuller and Henry Hedge must have talent in their associates. . . . I require genius and, if I find that, I do not need talent· and talent without genius gives me no pleasure." Emerson, *Journals*, V, 248.

22. See entry dated November, 1839, from Miss Martineau's diary, quoted by Mrs. Chapman in *Harriet Martineau's Autobiography* (Boston, 1877), II, 319. Also *Memoirs*, I, 192-94.

23. Chapman, *op. cit.*, I, 381.

24. *Margaret and Her Friends* (Boston, 1895).

25. Quoted in *Memoirs*, I, 349.

26. See article by W. M. Hess, "Conversations in Boston, 1839," *Catholic World*, CXLIX (June, 1939), 309-17.

27. *Memoirs*, I, 342.

28. *Ibid.*, p. 237.

29. MS letter in Fuller Papers, Boston Public Library. Reprint in *Memoirs*, II, 24-25, shows the usual editorial tampering of Emerson *et al.*

30. MS letter dated April 19, 1840, in Fuller Papers, Boston Public Library. Partially reprinted in *Memoirs*, II, 26-27.

31. MS letter dated July 5, 1840, in Fuller Papers, Boston Public

Library. Partially reprinted in Rusk, *Letters*, II, 309-10, and partially in Higginson, *Margaret Fuller*, pp. 154-56.

32. MS letter dated July 2, 1840, in Emerson Papers, Houghton Library. Reprinted in Rusk, *Letters*, II, 311.

33. MS letter dated Aug. 4, 1840, in Emerson Papers, Houghton Library. Reprinted in Rusk, *ibid.*, p. 322.

34. *Correspondence of Carlyle and Emerson*, I, 304.

35. Cooke, *An Historical and Biographical Introduction*, I, 75.

36. See letters dated Dec. 1, 1840, and Oct. 18, 1841, explaining Margaret's reasons for rejecting Thoreau's work in Harding and Bode, *The Correspondence of Henry David Thoreau* (Washington Square, 1958), pp. 41-42, 56-57.

37. Letter dated July 19, 1840, partially printed in Higginson, *Margaret Fuller*, pp. 157-58. Remainder printed in Rusk, *Letters*, II, 309-10.

38. *Memoirs*, II, 29.

39. MS letter dated Nov. 12, 1843, in Fuller Papers, Boston Public Library. Partially reprinted in Higginson, *Margaret Fuller*, pp. 166-67.

40. Manuscript in Fuller Papers, Boston Public Library. Reprinted in Higginson, p. 167.

41. MS letter dated Feb. 2, 1841, in Fuller Papers, Boston Public Library. Partially reprinted in Higginson, p. 162.

42. *Memoirs*, I, 323-24.

43. Octavius B. Frothingham, *George Ripley* (Boston, 1882), p. 86.

44. *Journals*, V, 473.

45. For her views of Ripley and his project, see MS letters dated May 31 and Oct. 28, 1840, in Fuller Papers, Boston Public Library. Latter partially reprinted in Higginson, *Margaret Fuller*, p. 180.

46. All quotations in this paragraph taken from letter dated Oct. 18, 1840, reprinted in *Memoirs*, II, 46.

47. MS letter dated Dec. 22, 1840, in Fuller Papers, Boston Public Library. Partially reprinted in *Memoirs*, II, 57. Letter dated March 29, 1841, partially reprinted in *ibid.*, pp. 58-59.

48. See Elizabeth Peabody's "Plan of the West Roxbury Community" in *The Dial*, II (January, 1842), pp. 361-72. Also Emerson's review of the *Social Destiny of Man*, I (October, 1840), 265; and "Fourierism and the Socialists," III (July, 1842), 86-96.

49. See Emerson's remarks concerning "Dolon," which appeared in *The Dial*, July, 1842; in Rusk, *Letters*, III, 63.

50. *American Note-Books*, p. 225.

51. MS letter dated June 4, [1842] in Henry W. and Albert A. Berg Collection, New York Public Library.

52. For the full details of this matter, see Frederick Fuller's "Haw-

thorne and Margaret Fuller Ossoli," *Literary World,* Vol. XVI (Jan. 10, 1885); also Anthony's *Margaret Fuller* (New York, 1920), p. 93.

53. MS letter dated Feb. 1, 1843, in Fuller Papers, Boston Public Library.

54. MS letter dated Oct. 27, 1843, in Fuller Papers, Boston Public Library. Badly mutilated fragment reprinted in *Memoirs,* II, 73.

55. *Ibid.,* p. 76.

56. *Memoirs,* I, 211.

57. MS letter dated Dec. 12, 1843, in Fuller Papers, Houghton Library. Reprinted in part in *Memoirs,* I, 224.

58. MS letter dated Oct. 2, 1841, in Fuller Papers, Houghton Library.

59. MS letter dated October, 1841, in Fuller Papers, Houghton Library. Reprinted in Rusk, *Letters,* II, 455-57.

60. MS letter in Fuller Papers, Boston Public Library. Partially reprinted in *Memoirs,* II, 58.

61. *Ibid.,* pp. 94, 96.

62. MS letter dated March 20, 1842, in Fuller Papers, Houghton Library.

63. Manuscript in Fuller Papers, Boston Public Library.

64. *Summer on the Lakes* (Boston, 1844), p. 62.

65. *Ibid.,* pp. 103-4.

66. *Ibid.,* p. 184.

67. MS letter dated Nov. 17, 1844, in Fuller Papers, Houghton Library. Reprinted in Rusk, *Letters,* III, pp. 269-70.

68. MS letter in Fuller Papers, Boston Public Library. Reprinted in Higginson, *Margaret Fuller,* pp. 201-2, and Wade, *Writings,* pp. 567-68.

69. *Journals,* VI, 364.

Chapter Four

1. See *Correspondence of Carlyle and Emerson,* II, 115. While admitting that Margaret Fuller had been well paid and honorably employed by *The Tribune,* Emerson writes Carlyle, "Still this employment is not satisfactory to me."

2. *Daily-Tribune,* Aug. 1, 1846. Reprinted in Arthur Fuller's *Life Without and Life Within* (New York, 1869), pp. 354-55.

3. See article on clairvoyance in July 23, 1845, edition of the *Daily-Tribune.* Also comments on the Seeress of Prevorst in *Summer on the Lakes,* pp. 133-65.

4. MS letter dated February, 1845, in Fuller Papers, Houghton Library. Reprinted in Wade, *Writings,* pp. 574-75.

5. *Memoirs*, II, 151.

6. MS letter dated Jan. 15, 1845, in Griswold Papers, Boston Public Library.

7. *Recollections of a Busy Life* (Boston, 1868), p. 175.

8. *Daily-Tribune*, Dec. 7, 1844. Reprinted in Wade, *Writings*, pp. 389-95.

9. *Daily-Tribune*, March 4, 1845. See excerpt entitled "Three Classes of Literature" in Wade, *Writings*, p. 230.

10. See "A Short Essay on Critics," *The Dial*, Vol. I (July, 1840). Reprinted in *Literature and Art* (New York, 1852), pp. 2-8. Also in Wade, *Writings*, pp. 223-29.

11. Review of *The Raven and Other Poems, Daily-Tribune*, Nov. 26, 1845. Reprinted in *Life Without and Life Within*, pp. 87-92. Also in Wade, *Writings*, pp. 398-403.

12. *Ibid.*

13. From "The Modern Drama," *The Dial*, IV (January, 1844), 313. Reprinted in *Literature and Art*, p. 107.

14. *Ibid.*, p. 101. See also review of Longfellow's "Poems," *Daily-Tribune*, Dec. 10. 1845, for statement of organic theory; also comment on Metres as the expression of a nation's spirit in *Tribune*, May 12, 1845.

15. See her Preface to *Literature and Art*, which explains her reasons for attempting to introduce the works of European genius to Americans.

16. *Daily-Tribune*, Feb. 1, 1845. Reprinted in Wade, *Writings*, pp. 301-11.

17. *Literature and Art*, pp. 58-99. Reprinted in Wade, *Writings*, pp. 312-46.

18. *Literature and Art*, Part II, pp. 122, 124.

19. See *Daily-Tribune*, Dec. 10, 1845.

20. *Literature and Art*, Part II, p. 132. Greeley reports that Margaret begged off from reviewing Longfellow's work because she was unsympathetic to Longfellow's standards. She finally consented when Greeley found it impossible to review Longfellow's work himself.

21. Lowell behaved somewhat childishly and even vindictively toward Margaret Fuller. See *Letters of James Russell Lowell*, ed. by Charles E. Norton (New York, 1894), 2 vols. Especially Vol. I, pp. 103, 128, 131, and 142.

22. See review of *Tales* in *Daily-Tribune*, July 11, 1845, and review of *Poems*, *ibid.*, Nov. 26, 1845.

23. *Ibid.*, April 4, 1846.

24. See Margaret Fuller's manuscript letters to Duyckinck dealing with publication matters in the Duyckinck Collection, New York Public Library.

25. Details of the love affair are to be found in *Love-Letters of*

Margaret Fuller 1845-1846 (New York, 1903.) Although Margaret asked Nathan to return her letters, he refused. In 1873, for reasons best known to himself, he felt compelled to reveal to the world "this sacred experience of her inmost soul" (*Ibid.*, p. 5). Record of negotiations regarding purchase of the letters is in Fuller Papers, Boston Public Library.

26. *Ibid.*, p. 21.

27. *Ibid.*, p. 94.

28. *Ibid.*, p. 172.

29. MS letter dated January, 1846, in Fuller Papers, Houghton Library.

30. *The Complete Works of Edgar Allan Poe,* ed. by Charles F. Richardson (New York, 1902), VIII, 316.

31. *Ibid.*, IX, 18.

32. See letter to Sarah Helen Whitman dated Oct. 18, 1848, in *The Letters of Edgar Allan Poe,* ed. by John W. Ostrom (Cambridge, 1948), II, 394.

33. *The Complete Works of Edgar Allan Poe,* IX, 7.

34. *Ibid.*, p. 8.

35. *Ibid.*, pp. 8, 13, 14.

36. For details, see William F. Gill, *The Life of Edgar Allan Poe* (New York, 1878), p. 322. Also, letter to Sarah Whitman, dated Nov. 24, 1848, in Ostrom, *op., cit.,* II, 406-9.

37. *Ibid.*, p. 356. Letter is dated Jan. 4, 1848.

38. *Ibid.*, p. 394.

39. *Ibid.*, p. 427. Letter is dated February 14.

Chapter Five

1. MS letter dated March 3, 1846, in Fuller Papers, Houghton Library.

2. Letter dated July 31, 1846, in *Correspondence of Emerson and Carlyle,* II, 114-17.

3. *Memoirs,* II, 172.

4. Quoted from notebook in Higginson's *Margaret Fuller,* p. 224.

5. See discussion of various types of contemporary psychotherapy—clairmativeness, dunamizing, etc.—in Margaret Fuller's article in *Daily-Tribune,* July 23, 1845.

6. *Love-Letters of Margaret Fuller,* p. 187.

7. On November 6, 1846, Nathan wrote again to Margaret expressing admiration for her "great, superior, and well stored mind"; but at the same time he refused to gratify her wish to have her letters back, claiming that he could not "part with things so dear, so suddenly." See MS letter in Fuller Papers, Houghton Library.

8. Her views on English royalty and its dilemma in trying to eradicate the inequalities of English society are remarkably similar to those expressed by her old mentor and friend, Dr. Channing. See especially *Correspondence of William Ellery Channing and Lucy Aikin*, ed. by Anna Le Breton (Boston, 1874).

9. "M. Fuller's Papers on Literature and Art," *op. cit.*, IV (Oct. 3, 1846), 401-3.

10. *Memoirs*, II, 185.

11. Letter dated March 2, 1847, in *Correspondence of Carlyle and Emerson*, II, 125.

12. Letter dated Dec. 26, 1846, in *Memoirs*, II, 191.

13. Letter dated Jan. 18, 1847, in *Memoirs*, II, 201.

14. Letter X in "Things and Thoughts in Europe," *At Home and Abroad* (New York, 1869), p. 195.

15. Letter dated Jan. 18, 1847, in *Memoirs*, II, 197.

16. *Ibid.*, p. 198.

17. Letter dated Jan. 18, 1847, in *Memoirs*, II, 201.

18. See Leopold Wellisz, *The Friendship of Margaret Fuller D'Ossoli and Adam Mickiewicz* (New York, 1847), pp. 16-38. See also Letters XXIII and XXIV to the New York *Daily-Tribune*, *At Home and Abroad*, pp. 306, 317-19. See also *Adam Mickiewicz* (New York, 1951), especially pp. 258-64.

19. MS letter to Mary Rotch dated May 23, 1847, in Fuller Papers, Houghton Library.

20. *Memoirs*, II, 205-6. Slightly different version in *At Home and Abroad*, p. 205.

21. Letter dated May 7, 1847, in *Memoirs*, II, 209.

22. See letter to Francis C. Shaw dated Oct. 25, 1847, reprinted in Wade, *Writings*, p. 576. See also rather extensive comments on American artists in Letter XXIX dated March 20, 1849, to the *Tribune* in *At Home and Abroad*, pp. 368-78.

23. Letter XV dated Aug. 9, 1847, in *At Home and Abroad*, p. 234.

24. Letter XVII dated Oct. 18, 1847, *ibid.*, p. 248.

25. See *Memoirs*, II, 141.

26. *Ibid.*, p. 140.

27. Letter dated Dec. 16, 1847, *ibid.*, p. 223.

28. Letter dated Dec. 20, 1847, *ibid.*, p. 224.

29. Letter dated Jan. 12, 1848, *ibid.*, p. 232.

30. See manuscript account in Fuller Papers, Boston Public Library. Reprinted in *Memoirs*, II, 281-93.

31. The argument advanced by Madeleine Stern in *The Life of Margaret Fuller* (New York, 1942), pp. 430-31, seems quite plausible in the light of all available evidence today.

32. MS letter dated Rome, April, 1848, in Fuller Papers, Boston Public Library.

33. See MS letter of Emerson from London dated April 25, 1848, in Emerson Papers, Houghton Library. Reprinted in Rusk, *Letters,* IV, 61-64. Also letter from Paris dated May 31, 1848, *ibid.,* pp. 78-79.

34. Letter XXIV dated April 19, 1848, in *At Home and Abroad,* p. 327. See also letter to Emerson dated May 19, 1848, in *Memoirs,* II, 239.

35. Letter dated June 22, 1848, *ibid.,* p. 243.

36. *Iibid.,* p. 244.

37. *Ibid.,* p. 294.

38. Letter dated Feb. 23, 1849, *ibid.,* p. 259. Richard's manuscript letter is in the Fuller Papers, Houghton Library.

39. *Memoirs,* II, 289.

40. See Lowell's letter to William Story dated March 10, 1848, in Henry James, *William Wetmore Story and His Friends* (Boston, 1903), I, 105.

41. See manuscript account of Mrs. Story's version of Margaret's experience in Fuller Papers, Boston Public Library.

42. MS letter dated Dec. 11, 1849, in Fuller Papers, Houghton Library.

43. See letter dated Oct. 17, 1849, in Rusk, *Letters,* IV, 168. Letter dated April 11, 1850, *ibid.,* pp. 198-99, is the last Emerson ever wrote to Margaret Fuller.

44. Copy of manuscript letter dated Oct. 16, 1849, in Fuller Papers, Houghton Library. Reprinted with slight changes in *Memoirs,* II, 316-17.

45. MS letter dated March 5, 1850, in Fuller Papers, Boston Public Library.

46. For the Brownings' references to Margaret Fuller, see *The Letters of Elizabeth Barrett Browning,* ed. by Frederic Kenyon (London, 1898), I, 459ff.; II, 59; *Letters of Robert Browning,* ed. by Thurman Hood (New Haven, 1933), pp. 31-32, 33. See also Margaret's letter to Evert Duyckinck dated May 23, 1847, in Duyckinck Collection, New York Public Library.

Chapter Six

1. See Volume I, No. 4 (April, 1841). Reprinted in *Literature and Art,* pp. 9-14.

2. For a readable summary of what American students of German philosophy actually took from German sources, see René Wellek,

"The Minor Transcendentalists and German Philosophy," *NEQ*, XV (December, 1942), 652-80.

3. Letter addressed to James F. Clarke (1836) in *Memoirs*, I, 168.

4. Portions of Margaret's "Credo" are reprinted in the *Memoirs*, II, 88-92; but they have been rearranged by the editors until the original, which is intact in the Fuller Papers, Boston Public Library, is barely recognizable. See Frederick Braun, *op. cit.*, for a corrected version.

5. Quoted from her "Credo," in *Memoirs*, II, 91.

6. *Ibid.*, p. 88.

7. MS letter dated January, 1849, in Fuller Papers, Boston Public Library.

8. A good survey of articles appearing in the *Examiner* is given in Frances Pedigo's unpublished master's thesis, *Literary Criticism in the Christian Examiner* (Chapel Hill, 1946). For overall view of the period, see William Charvat, *The Origins of American Critical Thought 1810-1835* (Philadelphia, 1936).

9. *The Dial*, I (July, 1840), 6, 7.

10. *Ibid.*, pp. 7, 8.

11. *Ibid.*, pp. 9, 10.

12. See Charvat, *op. cit.*, pp. 7-26, for an account of prevailing critical principles and practices.

13. "Poets of the People" in *Papers on Literature and Art*, Part II, p. 3.

14. *Ibid.*, p. 4.

15. "American Facts," New York *Daily-Tribune* (May 19, 1845). Reprinted in *Life Without and Life Within*, p. 109.

16. See "Poets of the People," *op. cit.*, pp. 1-21.

17. See review of "Romaic and Rhine Ballads," *The Dial*, III (October, 1842), 179.

18. For a carefully balanced estimate, see Roland Burton's article, "Margaret Fuller's Criticism of the Fine Arts," *College English*, VI (October, 1944), 18-23. See also bibliography for articles by McMaster and Wallace.

19. "A Record of Impressions," *The Dial*, I (July, 1840), 79.

20. See the letter that she wrote to Beethoven one evening after attending a program at the Boston Academy of Music. *Memoirs*, I, 232-34. See also her article on *Goethe* in *The Dial*, II (July, 1841), 30, 31.

21. *The Dial*, II (October, 1841), 49.

22. Francis Fetis, *Music Explained*. See *The Dial*, III (April, 1843), 533-34. This is typical of Margaret's getting sidetracked from a discussion of music itself to take up incidental matters like audience behavior.

23. See Poe, "The Literati," *op. cit.*, pp. 9-10, 12, 14.

24. See MS letter dated Aug. 23, 1844, in Fuller Papers, Houghton Library.

25. *Memoirs*, II, 152-53.

26. *Margaret Fuller* (Boston, 1883), p. 152.

27. MS letter dated February, 1839, in Fuller Papers, Houghton Library.

28. "Poetry and Imagination," *Letters and Social Aims*.

29. MS letter to Margaret Fuller dated January 5, 1843, Fuller Papers, Houghton Library; Emerson, Journals, VI (March 23, 1843), 369.

30. Charles Poore's review of Elizabeth Hardwick's *A View of My Own*, New York *Times*, Aug., 23, 1962.

31. Horace Gregory, "Wilde Playing Oscar's Part," *The Commonweal*, LXXVII (Dec. 7, 1962), 275.

Selected Bibliography

PRIMARY SOURCES

1. *Bibliographies*

CHIPPERFIELD, FAITH. *In Quest of Love: The Life and Death of Margaret Fuller*. New York: Coward-McCann, Inc., 1957, pp. 303-11. Primary material thoroughly covered; secondary sources unnecessarily widened.

Literary History of the United States, ed. by SPILLER, THORP, JOHNSON, and CANBY (New York: Macmillan, 1948), III, 522-25. *Bibliography Supplement*, ed., Richard M. Ludwig (1959).

STERN, MADELEINE. *The Life of Margaret Fuller*. New York: E. P. Dutton & Co., Inc., 1942. Extensive coverage in chapter bibliographies.

WADE, MASON. *The Writings of Margaret Fuller*. New York: The Viking Press, 1941, pp. 595-600. Chronological list of publications in the *Western Messenger, The Dial,* and New York *Daily-Tribune.*

2. *Texts*

Margaret Fuller's writings are now out of print except for *The Dial* and the excerpts in Perry Miller's *The Transcendentalists* (1950) and *The American Transcendentalists* (1957). No edition of her work has been published since Mason Wade's one-volume collection of *The Writings* (1941), and Wade's book is hard to find. It is invaluable as the only modern reprint of *Woman in the Nineteenth Century* and of an edited version of *Summer on the Lakes.*

The posthumous collections in *At Home and Abroad* (1856) and *Life Without and Life Within* (1859) are available only in a few libraries, and *Woman in the Nineteenth Century* (1845; later reprints) and *Papers on Literature and Art* (1846; later reprints) are rare. *Summer on the Lakes* (1844) is a collector's item.

Editions used in this study:

Art, Literature and The Drama, ed. by A. B. FULLER. Boston: Roberts Bros., 1889. Contains translation of Goethe's *Tasso* as well as papers on literature and art.

Selected Bibliography

At Home and Abroad or Things and Thoughts in America and Europe, ed. by A. B. FULLER. 3rd ed.; Boston: Crosby, Nichols and Co., 1856.

Conversations with Goethe . . . Translated from the German of Eckermann. Boston: Hilliard, Gray and Co., 1839. (Published as Vol. IV of *Specimens of Foreign Standard Literature,* ed. by GEORGE RIPLEY.)

Correspondence of Fräulein Günderode and Bettina von Arnim. Boston: Burnham, 1842 (translation).

The Dial: A Magazine for Literature, Philosophy, and Religion. 4 vols. New York: Russell & Russell, Inc., 1961. Contains many of Miss Fuller's most significant critical articles.

Life Without and Life Within, ed. by A. B. FULLER. Boston: Brown, Taggard and Chase, 1859.

Literature and Art. New York: Fowler and Wells, 1852.

Love Letters of Margaret Fuller, 1845-1846. Intro. by JULIA WARD HOWE. New York: D. Appleton, 1903.

Memoirs of Margaret Fuller Ossoli, ed. by R. W. EMERSON, W. H. CHANNING, and J. F. CLARKE. 2 vols. Boston: Phillips, Samson and Co., 1852. Contains lengthy excerpts from journals, correspondence, and manuscripts. Long out of print and still indispensable, this book is in large measure responsible for the distorted and wooden image of Margaret Fuller that overlays the warm and passionate nature of one of America's gifted daughters. Love's labors truly lost in the sentimental desires of three proper gentlemen to protect the memory of a "womanly woman" from herself.

Summer on the Lakes in 1843: Boston: Little and Brown, 1844.

Woman in the Nineteenth Century. Boston. John P. Jewett & Co., 1855.

The Writings of Margaret Fuller, ed. by MASON WADE.

3. *Manuscripts*

The Boston Public Library and the Houghton Library contain the important collections of Fuller letters, diary and journal excerpts. They have been used by courtesy of the Trustees of the Boston Public Library and the officials of Harvard University. The sources bowdlerized by Emerson, Channing, and Clarke and later partially recovered by T. W. Higginson for his biography of Margaret Fuller are located in the Boston Library while the Houghton contains a rich assortment of letters and memorabilia of Margaret and her family. The Emerson correspondence is also available here, both in manuscript and in Rusk's excellent edition. Though not in manuscript form, *The Letters of James Freeman Clarke to Margaret Fuller,* ed. by John W. Thomas (Hamburg, 1957) provides an authoritative primary record of a significant personal relationship.

SECONDARY SOURCES

The following selective list contains the biographical and critical writings most useful to the student of Margaret Fuller and her times.

Adam Mickiewicz-Poet of Poland, ed. by MANFRED KRIDE. New York: Columbia University Press, 1951. A symposium account of the Polish nationalist's relations with Margaret Fuller, Cooper, Emerson, *et al.*

ANTHONY, KATHERINE, *Margaret Fuller, a Psychological Biography.* New York: Harcourt, Brace and Howe, 1920. First of modern biographies. Contains shrewd insights but overemphasizes Freudian interpretation.

BRAUN, FREDERICK AUGUSTUS. *Margaret Fuller and Goethe.* New York: Henry Holt, 1910. Shows Miss Fuller's role as interpreter of German culture to America and emphasizes centrality of Goethean thought in her *Weltanschauung.*

BURTON, ROLAND C. "Margaret Fuller's Criticism of the Fine Arts," *College English,* VI (October, 1944), 18-23. Though perceiving basic issues in aesthetics, Miss Fuller never succeeded in rising above the "literary" approach to criticism of the arts.

CHIPPERFIELD, FAITH. *In Quest of Love: The Life and Death of Margaret Fuller.* New York: Coward-McCann, Inc., 1957. Most recent biography. Readable but indulges in imaginary conversations and rearrangement of primary materials. Sees subject as "arch-Romantic" heroine.

CLARKE, JAMES FREEMAN. *Autobiography, Diary and Correspondence,* ed. by Edward E. Hale. Boston: Houghton Mifflin Company, 1891. Valuable supplement to Thomas' edition of *Letters.*

COOKE, GEORGE WILLIS. *An Historical and Biographical Introduction to Accompany the Dial.* 2 vols. New York: Russell & Russell, Inc., 1961. Still the primary source of information about matters relating to editing and publishing of *The Dial.*

EMERSON, RALPH WALDO. *Journals,* ed. by E. W. EMERSON and W. C. FORBES. Boston: Houghton Mifflin Company, 1910.

————. *Letters,* ed. by RALPH L. RUSK. New York: Columbia University Press, 1939.

FROTHINGHAM, OCTAVIUS. *George Ripley.* Boston: Mifflin Company, 1882.

————. *Theodore Parker: A Biography.* Boston: James R. Osgood and Co., 1874.

————. *Transcendentalism in New England.* Harper Torchbook. New York: Harper & Brothers, 1959. Still a beginning point in any study of the broad aspects of this subject.

FULLER, FREDERICK T. "Hawthorne and Margaret Fuller Ossoli," *Literary World,* Vol. XVI (January 10, 1885). Spirited rejoinder to Hawthorne's criticism of Margaret Fuller in unpublished fragment of *French and Italian Notebooks,* later revealed to public gaze in Julian Hawthorne's *Nathaniel Hawthorne and His Wife.* Boston: Osgood, 1885.

GILL, WILLIAM F. *The Life of Edgar Allan Poe.* New York: W. J. Widdleton, 1878.

GODDARD, H. C. "Transcendentalism," *Cambridge History of American Literature,* ed. by TRENT *et al.* New York: The Macmillan Co., 1944, I, 326-48.

GREELEY, HORACE. *Recollections of a Busy Life.* Boston: H. Brown & Co., 1868. Tribute to "the most remarkable, and in some respects the greatest, woman whom America has yet known!"

HARASZTI, ZOLTÁN. "Brook Farm Letters," *The Bulletin of the Boston Public Library,* XII (February, 1937), 49-68; (March, 1937), 93-114.

————. *The Idyll of Brook Farm.* Boston: Public Library, 1937.

HAWTHORNE, NATHANIEL. *American Notebooks.* Boston: Osgood, 1868.

————. *The Blithedale Romance.* Boston: Osgood, 1852.

————. *French and Italian Notebooks.* Boston: Osgood, 1871.

HIGGINSON, THOMAS W. *Margaret Fuller Ossoli.* Boston: Houghton Mifflin Company, 1884. Does much to correct image of the *Memoirs* but is still too gentlemanly to be objective about personality conflicts.

JAMES, HENRY. *William Wetmore Story and His Friends.* 2 vols. Boston: Houghton Mifflin & Co., 1903. Contains interesting views of Margaret Fuller's Roman experiences by Lowell, James, and Story.

JONES, ALEXANDER E. "Margaret Fuller's Attempt to Write Fiction," *The Boston Public Library Quarterly,* VI (April, 1954), 67-73. Tells how one attempt at storytelling caused guilt feelings and led to her abandoning further attempts.

KING, BOLTON. *Mazzini.* London: J. M. Dent & Co., 1903. One of most readable and useful accounts of Margaret Fuller's "great man."

LONG, O. W. *Frederick Henry Hedge: A Cosmopolitan Scholar.* Portland, Maine: The Southworth-Anthoensen Press, 1940. Shows reciprocal influence of two disciples of German literature.

————. *Literary Pioneers.* Cambridge: Harvard University Press, 1935. Contains early studies of German influence on Americans like Edward Everett, George Bancroft, and Longfellow.

LOWELL, JAMES R. *Letters*, ed. by Charles E. Norton. 2 vols. New York: Harper & Brothers, 1894.

McMASTER, HELEN. "Margaret Fuller as a Literary Critic," *University of Buffalo Studies*, VII (December, 1928), 35-100. Balanced view of Miss Fuller's critical theory and practice. Tends to dismiss Poe's "minority report." Considers Margaret's criticism of music "ludicrous."

MILLER, PERRY. *The American Transcendentalists*. Garden City, N. Y.: Doubleday & Co., 1957.

————. *The Transcendentalists*. Cambridge: Harvard University Press, 1950.

PARTON, JAMES. *Life of Horace Greeley*. Boston: Osgood, 1867. An account by a man who lived and worked closely with Greeley.

POE, EDGAR ALLAN. *Letters*, ed. by JOHN W. OSTROM. 2 vols. Cambridge: Harvard University Press, 1948. Contains Poe's candid judgments of "Miss Fuller, that detestable old maid."

————. "The Literati" in *The Complete Works of Edgar Allan Poe*, ed. by CHARLES F. RICHARDSON. New York: G. P. Putnam's Sons, 1902, IX, 6-19.

RUSK, RALPH L. *The Life of Ralph Waldo Emerson*. New York: Charles Scribner's Sons, 1949. Useful companion to *Letters* and *Journals*.

SHEPARD, ODELL. *Pedlar's Progress: The Life of Bronson Alcott*. Boston: Little, Brown, 1937. Valuable portrait of an "uneasy" friend of Margaret Fuller as well as a rich tapestry of intellectual milieu of 1830's and 1840's.

SWIFT, LINDSAY. *Brook Farm*. New York: Macmillan, 1900. Still one of most authoritative treatments.

THOREAU, HENRY D. *The Correspondence of Henry David Thoreau*, ed. by Walter Harding and CARL BODE. Washington Square: New York University Press, 1958.

WADE, MASON. *Margaret Fuller: Whetstone of Genius*. New York: The Viking Press, 1940. By all odds the best biography. Scholarly thoroughness and readable style. Lack of apparatus makes identification of sources somewhat difficult. Unfortunately out of print.

WALLACE, MARGARET, "Margaret Fuller: Critic," *The Bookman* (March, 1929), pp. 60-67. Points out that Miss Fuller's "scientific method" suffered from lack of scientific knowledge. Emphasizes her crusade against insularity.

WARFEL, HARRY R. "Margaret Fuller and Ralph Waldo Emerson," *PMLA*, L (June, 1935), 576-94. Indicates fundamental differences in attitude toward problem of evil and nature of self-reliance.

WELLEK, RENÉ. "The Minor Transcendentalists and German Philosophy," *New England Quarterly*, XV (December, 1942), 652-80. Margaret Fuller's contacts with German philosophy not too happy. Her point of view closest to that of George Ripley among minor transcendentalists. Her major consideration aesthetic rather than technically philosophic.

WELLISZ, LEOPOLD. *The Friendship of Margaret Fuller D'Ossoli and Adam Mickiewicz.* New York: Polish Book Importing Co., 1947. Primary source of letters from Mickiewicz.

Index